Big Questions, Straight Answers

by David Hulme

Vision Media Publishing
Pasadena, California
2013

PUBLISHED BY VISION MEDIA PUBLISHING
P.O. Box 90607
Pasadena, California 91109-0607

Vision Collections are compiled and revised from material previously
published in the quarterly journal *Vision* (www.vision.org).

All scriptures are from the New King James Version (© 1988 Thomas
Nelson, Inc.) unless otherwise noted.

Cover art by Janette Saviano
ISBN 978-0-9822828-1-6

Contents

v   Introduction

1   Prologue: Turning Points

5   Of Weapons and Warfare

17   Interview: The New War?

23   The Violent Heart

35   "What Shall We Eat and Drink?"

44   Let Justice Be Done

52   Hot Evil, Cold Evil

56   Changing Human Nature

59   Missing The Mark

62   Why Suffering?

76   Finding God's Forgiveness

86   Interview: Hope Springs Eternal

97   Interview: The Many Faces of Forgiveness

110   A Change of Mind

114   Interview: Fusing Mind and Matter

124   Four Giant Steps for Mankind

126   Finding Peace of Mind

Introduction

Throughout history people have asked why, if God is both good and all-powerful, He doesn't intercede to prevent pain and suffering in the world. Why does He allow war, genocide and other atrocities? Why does He allow innocent people, especially children, to suffer at times?

Other vexing questions come to mind: Can we be forgiven? And how do we forgive others? Then there are the fears that come with everyday life: Will I be able to provide for my family? How do I achieve peace of mind and overcome anxiety? At the global level, we are faced with the fear of nuclear disaster, and we wonder if there is anything we can do to prevent the environmental ruin of the earth.

Answers to these kinds of questions are possible. Each issue of *Vision* magazine tries to make them known, as does this collection of essays and interviews from publisher David Hulme.

Uncertainty, fear, hardship and suffering are all realities of the human condition. Every generation has had to deal with them, and they are not going to go away as long as human nature prevails. But we can develop an understanding and a perspective that helps us find true peace of mind in spite of these realities.

Each of the following essays tackles some aspect of these big questions and offers another way of viewing them. It's not about hiding one's head in the sand or believing that ignorance is bliss. On the contrary, each article takes a practical look at the underlying causes of the big questions and problems humanity faces and offers workable solutions. At the heart of this alternative perspective is the conviction that the answers are spiritual in nature. Whether it is coming to acceptance of hardship and tragedy that is not one's fault, or finding a pathway out of a difficult trial caused by one's own failings, there is a change that must take place in the heart and mind. And in that realization lies the biggest question we face: Can I really change my human nature? Several of the concluding chapters in this book deal directly with that question. We think you will be encouraged by the answers.

Big Questions,
Straight Answers

Prologue:
Turning Points

"September 11" will need no year attached to it for us to relive the sickening realization that a terrorist's action can change our world in a heartbeat. In the hours following the attacks, many said nothing would ever be the same again. It was for most a kind of turning point, a hinge of history.

The idea that there are such critical turning points, moments when major, irreversible shifts take place, is a well-known concept. The invention of the printing press and the atomic destruction of Hiroshima and Nagasaki are obvious examples of the world taking unchangeable turns, some for the worse, others for the better.

Certainly what happened in New York, Washington and Pennsylvania stunned the entire world. For most, the effect was intensely personal: it could happen anywhere on an otherwise peaceful, sunny morning.

Charting just what changed as the door of history swung on its hinge that day is an instructive task.

A couple of days after the catastrophe, award-winning author Ronald Steel, writing in the *New York Times*, noted that what had changed most was America's perception of its invulnerability on its own shores. That myth, he said, had been shattered for good.

Others claimed that the United States had received and responded to "a wake-up call"—that the nation had been called to action and had responded with self-sacrifice, bravery, unity, compassion and appropriate introspection. Not since that other day of infamy more than 70 years ago at Pearl Harbor had the nation been galvanized in the same way. Certainly the higher-order attributes of human beings came to the fore in the face of this overwhelming tragedy. And not only in the United States. Around the world nations expressed their combined horror, sympathy and solidarity against the forces of depravity.

Yet the world itself, with its global communications, interdependence, complexity and plurality, is a vastly different place than it was in December 1941.

Noted military historian Sir John Keegan commented in London's *Telegraph* that sophisticated new weapons in the hands of coalition forces gave them great superiority over the enemy. An editorial in that newspaper observed: "Within three months of the suicide hijackings on September 11, the United States has brought a regime on the other side of the world to its knees. George Bush has shown that he can strike against the sponsors of terrorism at will." In other words, one of the things that changed is that terrorists cannot be assured that they will get away with their evil, even by hiding on the other side of the globe.

One other turning point that was mooted in the early aftermath of the terrorist attacks was a renewal of religious interest and commitment. It's true that the sale of Bibles increased significantly in the United States in the days and weeks following September 11. Church attendance also went up as people tried to come to terms with unfathomable destruction. Yet a survey revealed that, in the main, the new attendees were disappointed by their experience, finding few answers in the traditional churches. As a result, attendance soon slumped again. Who would explain the contents of those many new Bibles?

The most significant turning point for any human being is the moment when we acknowledge that we do not have the answers to the deepest questions of life. Tragedy has a way of bringing us face-to-face with ourselves. It is a great disappointment in such times to find that some of the presumed spiritual leaders have little help to give.

The answers to the questions of why there is evil in the world, and of where God is in such times of profound loss, are discoverable. Each issue of *Vision* magazine tries to make them known, as does this collection of essays and interviews.

Of Weapons
and Warfare

It is a fact that today's trillion-dollar defense industry had its beginnings only after World War II. There had been industrialized armaments production prior to and during the first great conflict of the 20th century, but on a small scale. It was the Nazi rise to power and the global Allied response to it that gave weapons manufacturers their cue. The ensuing Cold War between East and West, led by the U.S. and Soviet superpowers, guaranteed the expansion of arms production for decades to come.

The fact of continual widespread war during the next half century meant that the armaments industry itself would globalize and demand rapid technological development. This happened not only in the United States, the Soviet Union (later the Russian Federation) and Western Europe but also in China, India, Israel, South Africa and Brazil.

Despite the early 21st century's worldwide economic disruption, the 2012 report from the Stockholm International Peace Research Institute (SIPRI) put annual worldwide military expenditure for the previous year at $1.738 trillion—up about 118 percent since 2000.

A Complex Issue

In a world that yearns for disarmament and peace, warfare has become a globalized problem. The defense industry is a key element in the equation, answering the demands of military establishments and various governments that need jobs creation and the growth of defense-related exports to further domestic prosperity.

This raises fundamental moral questions, though not for the first time. Following World War II, American general Omar Bradley summarized the moral deficit that had emerged after that conflict. In 1948 he said, "The world has achieved brilliance without wisdom, power without conscience. Ours is a world of nuclear giants and ethical infants. We know more about war than we know about peace, more about killing than we know about living."

Despite Bradley's perceptive analysis, a wartime colleague, U.S. president Dwight D. Eisenhower (1953–61), oversaw the phenomenal postwar growth and development of the American military-industrial complex. Yet when it came time to step down from office, he too made a speech in which he warned about the dangers inherent in the relentless pursuit of supremacy by military-industrial means. He said, "In the councils of government, we must guard against the acquisition of unwarranted influence, whether sought or unsought, by the military-industrial complex. The potential for the disastrous rise of misplaced power exists and will persist."

Today the military-industrial complex is far more powerful and influential than Eisenhower could have imagined. SIPRI calculates the U.S. share of 2011 armaments purchases at 40.9 percent of the world's total. China comes a distant second at 8.2 percent! The reason usually given is that the United States has obligations worldwide, whereas other nations do not. While there have been ups and downs in spending and development over the past several decades, the future of the industry now seems to depend on five factors. According to military and defense analyst Richard Bitzinger, they are the hierarchical nature of the global arms industry, defense spending, the global arms market, the globalization of armaments production, and the emerging information technologies–based revolution in military affairs.

Let's look at them individually and assess the likelihood of a dramatic shift from involvement in globalized arms production to disarmament and universal peace.

Key Factors

Just a few primary actors affect the arms industry at the global level. In his 2009 book, *The Modern Defense Industry: Political, Economic, and Technological Issues*, Bitzinger reported that what was produced by the United States, the United Kingdom, France, Germany, Italy and Russia accounted for 85 percent of the world's armaments production at the time. These are the most influential players, with the largest output and the most money to spend on research and development. Others in the second, third or fourth tiers of the arms hierarchy may adapt and modify or copy and reproduce what these leaders do. They simply cannot compete. They must choose between the high cost of dependency and being left behind.

Because of the depth of commitment to defense industries in first-tier countries, it seems unlikely that they will become less viable. It is important to note the difficulty of uncoupling the arms industry from national prosperity and employment in such countries. According to SIPRI, the "strong relationship between arms producers and governments and the industry's perceived importance to national security . . . shield it from the immediate impact of severe economic downturns. This status is reflected in the continued high levels of arms sales, high profits, large backlogs and strong cash flows generated by arms production." If this is the case for those who produce 85 percent of armaments output, significant reduction in such production is unlikely.

The second factor identified by Bitzinger is the defense budgets of these and other nations, which are themselves affected by a variety of factors. They do not always increase. Major shifts in the geopolitical landscape, such as the collapse of the Soviet Union and the subsequent impact on those countries in its orbit, affect production and sales. The peace dividend associated with the end of the Cold War meant that many were laid off in defense-related industries, and arms producers consolidated or merged. But since the turn of the 21st century, spending increased again as long-planned projects came on line, the wars in Iraq and Afghanistan dragged on, and various East and South Asian nations boosted their spending levels. Budgets in the United States and Russia grew, while in Europe and Japan they were slow to static. China and India increased their expenditures for arms significantly. China reports that its defense spending rose at an average of nearly 10 percent per year between 1990 and 2005; its 2009 defense budget rose 14.9 percent over the previous year, according to Bitzinger. He noted that India's increase amounted to 37 percent between 2000 and 2007. Similar high percentages were recorded for Singapore and South Korea.

Third is that by no means all of the armaments produced by any nation are destined for its defensive purposes. In this global arms market, Bitzinger reports, weapons sold by several of the leading manufacturers in 2007 were destined primarily for export: Britain's BAE Systems (78 percent); France's Thales (75 percent) and Dassault (70 percent); and Sweden's Saab (68 percent). These figures are matched by those of manufacturers in Israel (75 percent) and Russia (80–90 percent) for the same general period. Though American firms have mostly sold to the domestic market, there has been an increase in exports, particularly of F-15 and F-16 fighters and M-1A1 main battle tanks. Many of these companies and their subsidiaries operate internationally, both producing and selling in countries other than their home base.

What these numbers tell us is that the arms bazaar is so intertwined, internationalized and interdependent that untangling it and making significant changes would be extraordinarily difficult.

A fourth and related factor is the move away from single-nation arms producers to transnational companies. It is not simply a matter of international investment but of joint ventures and cross-border mergers and acquisitions. This creates vulnerabilities in the event of serious conflicts. Nations cannot risk being held hostage by critical production facilities outside their borders. This is particularly true of the specialized parts needed for advanced technologies. The globalization of arms production also creates vulnerability in producer nations to rogue elements that may seek access to advanced technologies. Yet they are so critically needed by host country and producer alike that it is unlikely that they will scale back operations.

The fifth factor that inevitably affects the global arms industry is the continuing demand for improved weapons and systems. This is compounded by the fact that some fear that even the very nature of warfare is slated to change.

According to Bitzinger, the current revolution in military affairs is "nothing less than a paradigm shift in the character and conduct of warfare, and is thus seen as a process of discontinuous and disruptive (as opposed to evolutionary and sustaining) change." What he describes is network-centric warfare; that is to say, war fought with the aid of linked computers, sensors, microelectronics, miniaturization and related technology. This shift will demand responsiveness on the part of arms producers, and there is no reason to believe they will not comply. Indeed they already have. Witness the growth in the development and deployment of drone aircraft or unmanned aerial vehicles (UAVs), some for surveillance and others with the kill power of missiles.

Technological Revolution

The introduction of the Predator, Reaper and Global Hawk drones into the Iraq/Afghanistan/Pakistan theater changed the face of conflict. There are now thousands of such drones in operation. Often launched from distant air bases and guided by operators in faraway facilities, these weapons are really complete systems. According to the U.S. Air Force, "the MQ-1B Predator is a medium-altitude, long-endurance, unmanned aircraft system. . . . A fully operational system consists of four aircraft (with sensors and weapons), a ground control station, . . . a Predator Primary Satellite Link, . . . and spare equipment along with operations and maintenance crews for deployed 24-hour operations." The Reaper is a similar aircraft, while the larger Global Hawk is "a high-altitude, long-endurance unmanned aircraft system with an integrated sensor suite that provides intelligence, surveillance and reconnaissance, or ISR, capability worldwide."

Then there are the field-launched Shadow and the hand-launched Raven, thrown up into the air by soldiers to spy out what may be beyond the next hill or city block.

The next generation of drones, currently being tested, include some as small as insects that can fly in through windows, and others the size of commercial jets that can fly at very high altitudes. Loren B. Thompson of the Lexington Institute, a think tank in Arlington, Virginia, told the *Los Angeles Times* that drone technology "is the most hotly sought-after weapon system in a generation."

Undergoing tests is the new Global Observer. It has a wingspan equivalent to that of a medium-size passenger jet, is capable of surveying a nation the size of Afghanistan at one glance from as high as 65,000 feet (19.8 km), and can stay aloft for a week at a time.

The bat-winged, jet-powered X-47B will fly unmanned from an aircraft carrier, undetected by enemy radar, and return after carrying a payload of laser-guided bombs to its target. Having undergone its first test flight in early February 2011, the X-47B represents what some call "game-changing technology"; the use of such drones will mean engaging in combat from relatively safe distances, and while the goals will be no less destructive, human casualties could ostensibly be kept to a minimum.

These new craft represent the next generation of UAVs. Peter W. Singer, author of *Wired for War*, writes that by 2015 the U.S. army hopes "each brigade will actually have more unmanned vehicles than manned ones. . . . Each brigade will also have its own unmanned air force, with over a hundred drones controlled by the unit's soldiers."

Again, under these circumstances it is unlikely that the arms producers will cease their search for and production of new weapons of war. Singer speaks of his growing sense that "we are in the midst of something important, maybe even a revolution in warfare and technology that will literally transform human history."

Another View

As an aside to this new thrust in military-industrial thinking, Victor Davis Hanson notes that "even with changing technologies and ideologies, and new prophets of novel strategies and unconventional doctrines, conflict will remain the familiar father of us all—as long as human nature stays constant and unchanging across space and cultures." His summary statement is that "war is an entirely human enterprise" (*The Father of Us All: War and History, Ancient and Modern*, 2010). And here is our point of departure in considering the biblical dimensions of this global problem of warfare.

War as we know it is indeed an entirely human enterprise. But what is it in the heart of man that causes this perpetual descent into killing off another part of the species? Sometimes it is envy. In the first recorded murder in the first book of the Bible, a man kills his innocent brother "because his works were evil and his brother's righteous" (1 John 3:12). This is the apostle John's conclusion looking back over human history to that early time. In other words, there is right and wrong behavior toward our fellow man. One commentary says of Cain's behavior, "It is as if he could not wait to destroy his brother—a natural man's solution to his own failure." How often has envy played into one nation's aggression against others?

Another New Testament writer, James the brother of Jesus, asks, "Where do wars and fights come from among you?" His reply defines other aspects of human aggression: "Do they not come from your desires for pleasure that war in your members? You lust and do not have. You murder and covet and cannot obtain. You fight and war" (James 4:1–2).

It isn't that we fail to recognize the need for and the benefits of peace. There are many institutes devoted to the promotion of peace. Woodrow Wilson, perhaps the most idealistic of modern American presidents, worked tirelessly for the creation of the League of Nations. He devoted himself to the cause of peace. He was a highly intelligent, devoutly religious man. But he could not achieve his goal, despite the fact that other well-intentioned world leaders joined him.

Within 20 years after World War I, the entire planet was on the brink of terrible violence again. The war to end all wars was a forlorn hope.

The United Nations inherited its goals from the League. Outside its headquarters in New York stands a sculpture, a 1959 gift from the Soviet Union. On its base the ideal of peace is expressed in the words "We shall beat our swords into plowshares," taken from the prophetic book of Micah. More than half a century later, there has been little progress toward universal peace. No matter the idealism of human leaders, humanity can never seem to succeed in overcoming what seems like its death wish.

Does that mean peace can never come? Hanson would say not as long as we have human nature. But what did the prophet mean when he wrote, "They shall beat their swords into plowshares, and their spears into pruning hooks; nation shall not lift up sword against nation, neither shall they learn war anymore" (Micah 4:3)? Is this just senseless idealism? Or was he reflecting a divine imperative? Is it possible that a time is yet ahead for the planet when the end of war will be a reality—when people will simply not *learn* war?

Jesus of Nazareth came with a clear message of a coming time of universal peace on earth, when human nature would undergo transformation. He spoke of a future time of "regeneration" (Matthew 19:28). The apostle Peter made reference to a time of the "restitution of all things" (Acts 3:21, King James Version); and calling on the older prophets, Paul wrote of the mind that is set on "the things of the Spirit," which are "life and peace" (Romans 8:5–6). It was the prophet Jeremiah who had recorded God's words concerning the answer to human nature's downside: "I will put My law in their minds, and write it on their hearts" (Jeremiah 31:33). This is the way of transformation for the human heart, and it alone can lead to peace that is from then on willingly self-generated.

Can anything be done in the meantime? Like so many other problems common to humankind, the best place to start is at home, with you and me. The human mind can be individually renewed and made peaceful now. How? In the way that has been known for thousands of years. The same prophet that speaks of swords being beaten into tools of peaceful production explains, "He has shown you, O man, what is good; and what does the LORD require of you but to do justly, to love mercy, and to walk humbly with your God?" (Micah 6:8). That same God tells us, "The wisdom that is from above is first pure, then peaceable, gentle, willing to yield, full of mercy and good fruits, without partiality and without hypocrisy. Now the fruit of righteousness is sown in peace by those who make peace" (James 3:17–18).

SELECTED REFERENCES:

1 Richard A. Bitzinger (editor), *The Modern Defense Industry: Political, Economic, and Technological Issues* (2009).

2 Victor Davis Hanson, *The Father of Us All: War and History, Ancient and Modern* (2010).

3 Michael E. O'Hanlon, *The Science of War: Defense Budgeting, Military Technology, Logistics, and Combat Outcomes* (2009).

4 P.W. Singer, *Wired for War: The Robotics Revolution and Conflict in the 21st Century* (2009).

RELATED LINKS:

Stockholm International Peace Research Institute
http://www.sipri.org/

SIPRI is the Stockholm International Peace Research Institute, "an independent international institute dedicated to research into conflict, armaments, arms control and disarmament." The global think tank was established in Sweden in 1966 to commemorate that nation's 150-year record of unbroken peace. To this day it is partially funded by an annual grant from the Swedish government. This is a deep site, with multiple layers of pages devoted to various aspects of war and peace. In addition to its many online articles and databases on such subjects as regional and global security, armed conflict, conflict management, military spending, arms proliferation, and disarmament, SIPRI also offers an annual yearbook that brings together more comprehensive information for politicians, diplomats, analysts and interested members of the public.

Gallery: The Complete UAV Field Guide

http://www.popsci.com/technology/gallery/2010-02/
gallery-future-drones

Popular Science offers an online slide show highlighting an array of UAVs (unmanned aerial vehicles, or drones) being developed for or already in use by military forces around the world. From the hand-launched Raven to the stealth drone Phantom Ray to the miniature Samurai, the nature of warfare is being transformed in ways previously unimaginable. In addition to a photo or artist's rendition of each drone, "The Complete UAV Field Guide" provides details such as its manufacturer, size, habitat, behavior and notable features. You don't have to be especially interested in military matters to find this a fascinating and at the same time sobering presentation.

Interview:
The New War?

Sir John Keegan is widely regarded as the preeminent military historian of our time. In this interview with *Vision* publisher David Hulme, conducted soon after 9/11 (and well before the death of Osama bin Laden), he discussed the events of that day as well as the changing face of war. More than a decade later, his comments remain relevant and thought-provoking.

DH You have had a long and distinguished writing career as a war historian and as defense editor for the London *Telegraph*. What led you into the profession, and why did you choose it?

JK I didn't choose the profession, I was just interested from an early age in soldiers and what they did. I am a child of the Second World War. As a nine-year-old, I saw the preparations for D-day, which couldn't fail to fascinate. The countryside was swarming with soldiers and military equipment. I remember the morning of D-day very well indeed, and much more arrestingly, I remember the night of June 5–6, when the American airborne divisions—the 101st and the 82nd—flew to Normandy. It must have been the 101st that flew over my parents' house. The sky was full of aircraft taking the parachutists to Normandy—a most extraordinary sight, a most extraordinary noise.

So anyhow, there was that childhood experience which I think made me interested. I was also interested in history. When I went to Oxford I had to choose a special subject, and I chose military history. After I left Oxford, I didn't really know what to do, but I saw a job as a military historian at Sandhurst—a civilian lecturer. So I applied, and after a certain delay I was chosen. I spent 25 years at Sandhurst.

DH You talk about the planes going overhead, and how a highly impressive moment like that can change a person's life. In a way, September 11 must be that way for people. Someone said that no act of war ever had a larger audience.

JK I'm sure that's right, and indeed, I was one of the witnesses by televisual means, because I had come in to the *Telegraph*, and my taxi driver had said, "Something extraordinary is happening in New York. An airplane has flown into a skyscraper." When I arrived on the editorial floor, I found everybody watching a television. I sat down, and a few minutes later the second airplane flew into the second tower. So I was as much a witness as anybody else was of that ghastly event.

It left an image that recurs and will recur. I think it is one of the most dreadful things, because we are so used to skyscrapers and we are so used to airliners, so watching an airliner fly into a skyscraper has a most peculiar effect. It was the most widely witnessed act of war ever perpetrated and therefore highly sensational.

DH After September 11, it was suggested that we are hearing from a part of the world about what it is they perceive we have done to them.

JK I don't accept any of that. It was an appalling outrage and atrocity, and nothing in the relationship between the rich world and the Third World justified it at all. Most of the people who died in the Twin Towers disaster were not investment bankers going to work in stretch limousines. There was a huge restaurant on the top of the North Tower, so there were poor little waitresses and busboys and short-order cooks earning $8 an hour and living in Queens. They were worse off than these well-educated Arab graduates who had been to Hamburg University and who flew the airplanes. The attempt to justify September 11 in terms of disparity of wealth between America and the Third World is revolting! It's evidence of the corruption of the intellect—of the Western intellectual.

DH Is that corruption mirrored in the mind of Osama bin Laden?

JK Bin Laden is clearly not psychologically normal. He is the sort of intellectual who, if and when they manage to get their hands on power, do the most terrible things to those around them. Lenin, Stalin, Hitler, Pol Pot—he is one of them. He is a mass murderer. He is potentially a far greater mass murderer—one with an ideology that he believes justifies his urge to mass murder.

DH A lot of people have said that September 11 was the day the world changed, and certainly it changed in some ways. Do you feel it's a bit of an overreaction to state it that way?

JK I don't think the world changed in the way that it changed, say, with the end of the Nazi regime in 1945, or with the fall of communism in 1989. But it's changed in a more pervasive and I think unpleasant way. The end of communism was a good thing; the fall of Hitler was a good thing. It's more like the dropping of the atomic bomb, which altered forever the way states could behave toward each other. It's beginning already, because the benevolent regime of civil liberty that we are so used to in the West is now in retreat. All sorts of restrictions on powers of arrest, on privacy of personal information, and all the other things we associate with being free people, particularly in Anglo-Saxon countries, are already being eroded—and I think are going to be eroded further.

DH What is your perspective on the threats facing the world today?

JK Like everybody else, my ideas have been severely shaken by September 11. I was a believer in the new world order. I thought that a rational atmosphere of goodwill was the dominant influence after the fall of communism. But I was wrong. There is much less goodwill and rationality than one had thought. I still can't see a large-scale war as a likely development. Clearly al-Qaeda would love a large-scale war as long as they were behind it. But I can't see any large, organized state wanting a large-scale war now any more than before September 11. In that sense the idea behind the new world order is probably still operative. India and Pakistan are restrained by their possession of nuclear weapons. I can't see why China wants to fight anybody. The last thing Russia needs is a war. America certainly doesn't want a large-scale war. Nobody in Europe wants a war. Where else can you see a war? There are these wars in Africa, but they are struggles between bandits and warlords, not what we are talking about. That has to do with local power and personal enrichment.

DH You're not saying the end of war, but the end of war as we have known it?

JK War isn't useful to states any longer. That is the point. War is far too costly.

DH You have seemed to resist defining war. You have said, "War is collective killing for some collective purpose. That is as far as I would go in attempting to describe it."

JK Yes, but this is a bit of a personal argument on my part. During the Cold War it became an article of faith, particularly in the United States, that war is always a political act. I always thought that underestimated the violence factor. I've always thought that a lot of people involved in war simply like violence for its own sake or get caught up in violence for its own sake, and that it is dangerous and limiting to think of war as a political activity, pure and simple. And oddly, I think September 11 demonstrates the force of that point of view. Al-Qaeda doesn't seem to me to be a political organization at all. And those who took part, those who committed the atrocity, clearly weren't motivated by any motive you can call political. Politics must ultimately be a rational activity, and if you are prepared to kill yourself, you are indulging in something that is highly irrational. So that's further evidence to me that it is very, very dangerous to define the nature of war too closely. I think war can take many forms and does indeed mutate, rather as a virus mutates. I don't know how much further it can mutate beyond September 11. That seems to me almost an ultimate form of mutation.

DH Are you prepared to define war any further?

JK Well, peace is the absence of war, obviously. That used to be the only way in which peace was defined, but I think we are moving toward a larger, more generous definition. Peace should comprehend a positive spirit of cooperation between nations.

DH Beyond that, is peace a state of mind?

JK   Well, of course it is, but how often does the individual achieve a peaceful state of mind? How often do we relax? We've always got something to worry about. Peace of mind is a very elusive quality.

DH   What is your view of human nature?

JK   On the one hand we are told we are made in the image of God, and therefore there is something very, very good about us. We are equally told we have a fallen nature and there is something very bad about us. Therefore there is a conflict between the good and the bad in us. Indeed, if you have that view, you feel it every minute of your existence. But outside the individual is the same conflict.

DH   Does September 11 convince you that war is changing?

JK   Yes, I'm afraid it does. It is an exact example of this nasty tendency of war to mutate and to take a new viral form, which we don't have the antidote to. The viral analogy is particularly appropriate with al-Qaeda, because we don't know the extent of the conspiracy; we don't know the composition of the conspiracy—not in detail; we don't know the location of the conspiracy. It is exactly like a very nasty disease. We know it's there because we are afflicted by it, but we can't completely identify the nature of the infective agent.

DH   We throw our latest technology against it, yet we seem to be locked in a battle between something that is medieval and yet very, very modern.

JK   Unfortunately human beings are the most effective instruments of war ever invented. I mean, can you think of anything nastier than a graduate of the University of Hamburg who believes that God has told him to crash an airliner full of innocent people into a skyscraper full of innocent people? That is just about as nasty as you can get.

The Violent Heart

Woodrow Wilson, the 28th president of the United States, was perhaps the most idealistic of modern American presidents. Though he led his country against Germany toward the end of World War I, he did so only after resisting war as the preferred option. He then developed his famous Fourteen Points, which convinced the German government to lay down arms without admitting defeat.

At the 1919 Paris Peace Conference, Wilson worked for the creation of the League of Nations to promote peaceful international relations. For his efforts he was awarded the Nobel Peace Prize later that year.

A highly intelligent, devoutly religious man, Wilson devoted himself to the cause of peace. But he could not achieve his goal. Not only did the Senate reject U.S. entry into the League of Nations, but within 20 years of the war's end the entire world was in the grips of terrible violence again. "The war to end all war" proved to be a forlorn hope, and the League of Nations a failed instrument. Though a subsequent generation of leaders was able to forge the League's successor, the United Nations, the goal of preventing war remains unfulfilled to this day. It seems that no matter the highest of ideals set forth by leaders, humanity has never succeeded in overcoming what appears to be a death wish.

You may not have thought of it in such stark terms. Yet can any of us deny the legacy of violence that defined the last century?

This is the subject of Jonathan Glover's *Humanity: A Moral History of the 20th Century.* Glover is a professor of ethics at King's College, London. His book focuses on the violence of the past 100 years, dealing in particular with "the psychology which made possible Hiroshima, the Nazi genocide, the Gulag, the Chinese Cultural Revolution, Pol Pot's Cambodia, Rwanda, Bosnia and many other atrocities."

While this appalling list reminds us of how much mass violence has dominated the modern world, the *purpose* of the book harks back to the perhaps paradoxical desire humans have to overcome the violence within us. The book's message, writes Glover, "is not one of simple pessimism. We need to look hard and clearly at some monsters inside us. But this is part of the project of caging and taming them."

But while we may know the problem, the cure for the disease is far from us.

Violence From Beginning to End

There is much more than the last century to consider when it comes to the history of violence, of course. According to Glover, "it is a myth that barbarism is unique to the twentieth century: the whole of human history includes wars, massacres, and every kind of torture and cruelty."

In light of that statement, it is significant how often violence is referenced in the Bible, literally or conceptually, at critical junctures in earth's history.

The prophets Isaiah and Ezekiel both tell us of an angelic being who became corrupt before the arrival of humans on the earth. Isaiah refers to this being with the Hebrew *heylel* ("shining one" or "morning star," translated in English as "Lucifer" or "Light Bearer" from the Latin *lux*, *lucis*, "light"). No longer an angel of light, he had become an agent of darkness. Thereafter he is identified in the Bible as the Accuser or the Adversary (in Hebrew, *satan*). Ezekiel shows that violence became one of the tools of his trade. As a result of his corruption, he became dominated by aggression: "Your great wealth filled you with violence, and you sinned. So I banished you from the mountain of God. I expelled you, O mighty guardian, from your place among the stones of fire" (Ezekiel 28:16, New Living Translation). Satan was consumed by a violent attitude.

Not surprisingly, his entry into the human world led to further corruption. The Genesis account of his deception of humanity's parents is well known. By their actions, Adam and Eve did violence against their creator and suffered the penalty of banishment from Eden, the garden of God.

It wasn't long before the first recorded murder occurred, the first act of violence against a family member: Adam's son Cain struck down his brother, Abel. It was the beginning of a succession of violent acts. One of Cain's descendants, Lamech, was also a murderer, the biblical record indicating that he showed less remorse for his sin than Cain did.

By the sixth chapter of Genesis, we read that early human society had gone far downhill in respect of violence: "Then the LORD saw that the wickedness of man was great in the earth, and that every intent of the thoughts of his heart was only evil continually. And the LORD was sorry that He had made man on the earth, and He was grieved in His heart. . . . The earth also was corrupt before God, and the earth was *filled with violence*. So God looked upon the earth, and indeed it was corrupt; for all flesh had corrupted their way on the earth" (verses 5–6, 11–12, emphasis added throughout).

When we come to the much later New Testament Gospel accounts, we read of Jesus looking into the distant future and warning of a time of ultimate violence. It will be a time of such catastrophe that it will never be repeated: "For that will be a time of greater horror than anything the world has ever seen or will ever see again. In fact, unless that time of calamity is shortened, the entire human race will be destroyed. But it will be shortened for the sake of God's chosen ones" (Matthew 24:21–22, NLT).

This prophetic statement from Jesus accords with others in the book of Revelation, which says that, at the end of the age, Satan and his fallen followers will once again have their part to play in stirring up violence. Revelation 16:14 (NLT) tells of "miracle-working demons [causing] all the rulers of the world to gather for battle against the Lord on that great judgment day of God Almighty." Thankfully, as we see in the above passage from Matthew's Gospel, God will not allow the annihilation of humanity.

The Spirit of Violence

Though violence has stained human history from the beginning and, according to the Scriptures, will continue to mar it to the end of this age, Jesus proclaimed a very different world: a coming godly kingdom of peace. His message assures us that violence does not have to be an *individual* choice in today's violent world. But it takes understanding and effort to take a different course.

Sadly, we do not always realize the impact that the world we inhabit has on us. On one occasion Jesus had to explain to His own disciples that their attitude was very far from His own. He was on His way to Jerusalem, passing through a Samaritan village en route. When the Samaritans spurned Him, two of His disciples offered to call down fire from heaven to consume them. "But [Jesus] turned and rebuked them, and said, 'You do not know what manner of spirit you are of'" (Luke 9:52–55).

The disciples no doubt thought that they were quite right in what they had suggested, so Jesus' response must have shocked them. But the solution that seemed right to the disciples would have been a violent act that showed neither mercy nor understanding.

What spirit were they of? The Bible shows that there is a spirit in men and women that makes us unique and different from animals. The human brain is qualitatively different from the animal brain.

But there is more to this spiritual equation. The Bible also reveals that there are two other spiritual minds with which the human mind can interface, causing us to think in varied ways—for good or evil, for right or wrong (1 Corinthians 2:12). One spirit, the apostle Paul said, is of this world; the other is of God. Paul also showed that the world in general falls under the influence of a wrong spirit: "You used to live just like the rest of the world, full of sin, obeying Satan, the mighty prince of the power of the air" (Ephesians 2:2, NLT). He mentions that this being is "the god of this age" (2 Corinthians 4:4), who blinds people.

From what we know already of the Adversary's role in human history, we should not be surprised at the result when the human mind interfaces with the wrong spirit. Sadly, one of the depravities of the human mind when it combines with the spirit of the world, the spirit of disobedience, is violence. The disciples who wanted to call down destruction on others were operating according to that spirit.

A Line Through the Heart

Centuries later, recognizing the almost natural human proclivity for violence, Russian author Fyodor Dostoyevsky wrote that "people sometimes speak of man's 'bestial' cruelty, but this is very unfair and insulting to the beasts: a beast can never be so cruel as a man, so ingeniously, so artistically cruel." His comment takes us to another level in our consideration of violent behavior.

For some reason, the glorification of cruelty and violence preoccupies this present world. Box office attractions center on unspeakable violence. Not so long ago, for instance, many people flocked to see the long-awaited sequel to a gruesome movie about a serial killer. Part Two revealed a sometimes sympathetic portrait of a sadist who ate parts of his victims while they were still alive. Film critics recommended that people not take their children to see the movie with its profoundly disturbing scenes. But did you ever wonder why so many are inclined to view such horror in the first place?

Noting that "the festival of cruelty is in full swing," Glover asks: "What is it about human beings that makes such acts possible?"

Answering his own question, he says, "Three factors seem central. There is a love of cruelty. Also, emotionally inadequate people assert themselves by dominance and cruelty. And the moral resources which restrain cruelty can be neutralized. . . . Deep in human psychology, there are urges to humiliate, torment, wound and kill people."

Glover notes that his assertion echoes the words of the late Russian author Alexander Solzhenitsyn, who wrote about his experiences in Siberian exile in *The Gulag Archipelago*. Reflecting on the slender difference between guards and prisoners, Solzhenitsyn said: "If only it were all so simple! If only there were evil people somewhere insidiously committing evil deeds, and it were necessary only to separate them from the rest of us and destroy them. But the line dividing good and evil cuts through the heart of every human being. . . . It is after all only because of the way things worked out that they were the executioners and we weren't."

The Bible's revelation about the hidden nature of man provides the answer to this age-old question of what it is that propels humans into shocking, senseless violence from time to time. In a powerful comment on the way we can become, Isaiah wrote: "They spend their time plotting evil deeds and then doing them. They spend their time and energy spinning evil plans that end up in deadly actions. . . . *Violence is their trademark.* . . . Wherever they go, misery and destruction follow them. *They do not know what true peace is* or what it means to be just and good. They continually do wrong, and *those who follow them cannot experience a moment's peace*" (Isaiah 59:4–8, NLT).

In the Service of God?

Returning again to the New Testament, we find that even the most outwardly religious people can have a violent heart. After all, many of those who persecuted and plotted the unspeakably cruel death of Jesus Christ were devoutly committed to their religion. Clearly, religious belief is no indication of a right spirit.

In fact, Jesus said that the time would come when "whoever kills you will think that he offers God service. And these things they will do to you because they have not known the Father nor Me" (John 16:2–3). That is to say, such persecutors are out of sync with the mind of God but tuned in to another mind.

Even the apostle Paul took part in the persecution and death of Jesus' followers before his conversion. Acts 8:3 tells us that "he made havoc of the church, entering every house, and dragging off men and women, committing them to prison." Why did he do it? Because of entirely misplaced religious conviction.

Paul had to have it *revealed* to him that his violence was not something from the mind of God. Despite his religious zeal for God, he was as far from God as he could have been. He was under the influence of the wrong spirit.

And Now to You and Me

Quite rightly at this point you might be saying to yourself, "But I've never done anything like that. I've never assaulted or murdered anyone." But violence starts somewhere short of the act of murder, sometimes a long way short of that final act.

Most people have never considered that violence isn't simply attacking people physically. We do violence to each other when we allow Satan's adversarial state of mind to become our own. Remember that he is the spirit being who is centered on doing harm to human beings in any way he can. Sometimes, therefore, we commit an act of violence simply by what we say to others, or do to them, short of the act of murder.

Paul described himself as having been "a man of violence" prior to his conversion (1 Timothy 1:13, New Revised Standard Version). Alternative translations say he was "insulting," "arrogant," "an insolent overbearing man" or "a violent aggressor." The result was that he engaged in the persecution to death of early Christians. The point is that thoughts and attitudes precede action.

Jesus also had something to say about the state of mind that precedes physical violence: "You have heard that it was said to those of old, 'You shall not murder, and whoever murders will be in danger of the judgment.' But I say to you that whoever is angry with his brother without a cause shall be in danger of the judgment. And whoever says to his brother, 'Raca!' [an Aramaic term of contempt] shall be in danger of the council. But whoever says, 'You fool!' shall be in danger of hell fire" (Matthew 5:21–22).

Jesus was interested in the underlying attitude behind the final act of murder. It starts with things that are very familiar territory to us: insults, being "lightly angry" without a cause, calling someone an idiot, saying someone is worthless. It can end up in cruelty, terror, torture and murder.

There are other, more subtle ways in which we display a violent heart. We do violence to each other when we take up the sword of gossip. We can excuse ourselves by insisting we are only passing on information that someone else gave us. Yet the scriptural rules are quite clear: "Do not spread slanderous gossip among your people. Do not try to get ahead at the cost of your neighbor's life, for I am the LORD" (Leviticus 19:16, NLT). God says that "death and life are in the power of the tongue" (Proverbs 18:21). We do violence to a relationship when we spread gossip, *even if it is true*, or when we slander someone. Interestingly, in a clue to slander's origin, the Hebrew for "slanderer" is also *satan*.

So we can define violence in terms of slander, gossip, insolence or anger. But in what might seem like a contradiction, we can even be violent by being passive. We can disrupt what should be a right relationship by *failing* to respond in a godly way. This means that the practice of passive resistance is very much open to question.

The Moral Core

How, then, do we begin to come to terms with the violence that seems so naturally a part of us? There is no question that understanding what we are up against in the spirit world is central. A strong sense of personal moral identity is also a key. Knowing who we are morally cannot be underestimated. This speaks to the early and continuous formation of character: knowing what is right and exercising the will to do it. Glover writes, "The sense of moral identity is one relevant aspect of character. Those who have a strong sense of who they are and of the kind of person they want to be have an extra defence against conditioning in cruelty, obedience or ideology."

He continues: "Sometimes people's actions seem to be disconnected from their sense of who they are. This may be because they slide into participation by imperceptible degrees, so that there is never the sense of a frontier being crossed. This gentle slide can be a feature of the training of torturers. It was what the Nazis aimed at in securing collaboration in occupied countries. With the atomic bomb, the slide was gradual from making it only as a deterrent against Hitler to making it for actual use against Japan."

We must be careful that we do not become participants in cruelty or violence *gradually*. A well-formed personal moral identity should prevent it, but we sometimes allow ourselves to be compromised. Vigilance about our state of mind is essential.

A Violent World Comes to Rest

How can we become nonviolent people in the fullest sense? Hebrews 12:14 advises the followers of Jesus to *"pursue peace* with all people, and holiness, without which no one will see the Lord."

Part of pursuing peace is to treat people as people, not as commodities to be used up; to give people mental and spiritual space, just as we want it for ourselves. It is certainly to avoid coercing people in everyday life. The New Testament writer James said that "the fruit of righteousness is sown in peace by those who *make* peace" (James 3:18). Peacemaking is an active process. It requires action based on right principles. Living the right way and keeping God's law in respect of human relationships leads to peace and reconciliation. These are actions we can take now as we endeavor to come under the direction of the Spirit of God—the Spirit that binds our human mind to the mind of God. Those who are willing to take up the challenge of living now under God's rule experience peace as a foretaste of what is yet ahead for all of humankind.

God will set His hand to save humanity from its own ultimate act of aggression. At that time the violence of this world in all of its manifestations will end. The day is coming when, according to the book of Revelation, "the great dragon [will be] cast out, that serpent of old, called the Devil and Satan, who deceives the whole world." Finally Satan will be restrained, his influence removed. A new chapter will be added to the history of violence, signaling its effective control. The world's new condition will be peace and security through the practice of the law of God's love on all levels.

RELATED ARTICLES AT WWW.VISION.ORG:

"Taming the Monster Inside Us": An interview with Jonathan Glover

"Woodrow Wilson: Making the World Safe for Democracy"

"Family Violence"

"Who Am I? The Question of Youth Violence"

"What Shall We Eat and Drink?"

International agencies calculate that nearly a billion people go hungry every day. What will it take to solve global issues such as the problem of inadequate food and freshwater in vast regions of the world?

A child dies from hunger-related causes every six seconds— "the world's largest tragedy and scandal," says Jacques Diouf, director-general of the United Nations Food and Agriculture Organization (FAO). At the same time, about eight out of ten of the world's population live in areas where freshwater is under threat. Without adequate freshwater supplies, food cannot be produced.

Sounding the alarm, the World Economic Forum's "Global Risks" report for 2011 highlights the critical nature of "the food-water-energy nexus." The anticipated 30–50 percent rise in demand for all three resources over the next two decades could bring environmental disruption, political instability and geopolitical conflict. Population growth and increasing prosperity are exerting pressure on resources that in all probability cannot be withstood without coordinated strategies that address each part of the nexus. If nothing is done, the potential for disastrous consequences looms.

Goals and Challenges

Our concern in this article is with the securing of life at its most basic, in terms of the universal need to eat and drink every day. Security relates to more than protection of states against aggression. At the individual level, in addition to food and water, it includes unpolluted sustainable environments as well as protected communities based on equality, good health, safe childbirth, economic viability, and access to shelter and clothing.

The 2000 UN Millennium Declaration lists eight goals that relate to these human security concerns. But the primary Millennium Development Goal (MDG1) is to reduce by half, between 1990 and 2015, the number of undernourished and poverty-stricken people throughout the world. Although the UN reports that the picture has improved, they add that "even at the current rate of progress, estimates indicate that about 1 billion people will still be living on less than $1.25 a day in 2015—corresponding to a global extreme poverty rate of just below 16 per cent" ("The Millennium Development Goals Report, 2012"). Similarly, as of 2010 (the latest figures available) the 1996 World Food Summit's target required freeing another 500 million people from hunger by 2015. While some progress has been made—mostly in China and India according to an April 15, 2011, World Bank report—the reality is that even if the effort succeeded, almost half a billion would still go hungry every day.

Diouf notes that "the level of hunger makes it extremely difficult to achieve not only the first MDG but also the rest of the MDGs." Part of the difficulty arises from the potential volatility of food prices accentuated by natural disasters, severe weather, surging fuel costs, and uncoordinated government actions to protect domestic supplies. Then there's the demand for biofuels made from agricultural feedstocks, such as ethanol from corn/maize and other crops, that may play a significant role in food price volatility if oil supplies become disrupted. Over the next decade food prices are expected to rise and to remain at levels higher than during the first 10 years of this century.

The earth's water supply is finite. About 97 percent of it is brine and 3 percent is fresh. Of the freshwater, only 1 percent is accessible; the rest is trapped as ice and glaciers. Agriculture accounts for 70 percent of the freshwater consumed. But without radical changes in eating patterns, this percentage will rise. Both population and meat consumption in developing countries are on the increase. Industrialized meat production is far more water-intensive than grain production. Thus more stress will be placed on water resources in the years ahead. Added to this is the reality of already unsustainable water use in China, India and the United States. Demands will also increase on the energy front, and they, too, are dependent on freshwater.

But there is more to the water crisis. According to the Water Integrity Network (WIN), corruption is found at all levels of the water delivery system. Bribes are often required (and paid) for contracts; people are forced to pay illegal fees for connection to water supplies; and funds are diverted away from projects. WIN's Global Corruption Report 2008 notes that corruption in the water sector could inflate the costs of achieving the MDG target for water and sanitation by nearly $50 billion.

Just how compromised the water business can become is evident in the history of Southern Africa's Lesotho Highlands

Water Project—a massive undertaking accelerated in the 1990s with a planned cost of more than $8 billion. Funded in part by the World Bank, the project became mired in corruption. In well-publicized trials in Lesotho, Canadian, French and German multinationals were fined following conviction of bribery in the winning of contracts. The courts alleged that more than $6 million in bribes had been passed along to the local executive in charge of the project, who is now serving 15 years in prison. Irregularities in water projects have also been noted in case studies involving China, Kenya, Indonesia, Bolivia, Chile, Kazakhstan and Uganda. In the Chinese case, corrupt officials simply ignored environmental standards. As a result, 700 million people were receiving water polluted with human and animal waste.

The Will to Succeed

Despite the challenges to provide adequate food and water, UN secretary-general Ban Ki-moon believes that it is possible to empower the poorest countries and others limited by disease, isolation and internal strife to achieve all eight MDGs, because "the world possesses the [necessary] resources and knowledge." Indeed, in September 2010 several nations, institutions and companies made commitments to meeting the goals. With respect to MDG1, aimed at reducing hunger and poverty, the World Bank pledged to increase its annual financial support to $6–8 billion between 2010 and 2013. The Republic of Korea promised $100 million to help food security and agriculture programs. MDG7 (Ensure Environmental Sustainability) gained commitments from WaterHealth International for 75 water purification plants in Bangladesh and for extending water access to an additional

100 Indian villages, thus providing for 175,000 people, while PepsiCo agreed to provide clean water for 3 million people by 2015.

These are commendable actions, and there are, of course, other success stories to be emulated. Armenia, Brazil and Nigeria have encouraged small-scale food production at the individual level. This has alleviated hunger among some of the rural poor, who account for the majority of the world's undernourished. In three large American and Australian agricultural areas, increased efficiency has demonstrated what can be done to reduce water usage. In this context, according to water resource experts Peter Rogers and Susan Leal, "a 10 percent improvement in agricultural water use would free up more water than is currently used by all the cities and industries across the globe" (Running Out of Water).

The International Water Management Institute's (IWMI) survey of the world's agricultural needs from 2007 to 2050 concluded that while there are sufficient land and water resources to feed the world's growing population, immediate action to improve agricultural water use is essential to meet those needs. The IWMI is a research center supported by the Consultative Group on International Agricultural Research (CGIAR), a network of 60 entities including governments, international organizations and private foundations. But the question remains whether the global community will do enough to rise to the occasion. Tony P. Hall, a former U.S. ambassador to the UN Agencies for Food and Agriculture in Rome, was reported recently as saying of world hunger, "We have the ability to stop it, but do we have the will? It's a question of economic, political and spiritual will. So far, we've not shown it."

From where does spiritual will come? If the solution to the level of problem that is being raised here is indeed in part spiritual, then it must come from outside our physical world. Certainly the problems of corruption are widespread, and self-interest is endemic among humanity. What is needed is outside spiritual intervention and a fundamental change in human nature. It will take this kind of "breakthrough" to resolve the deeply entrenched problems that arise from the human heart. Despite our best efforts, finding complete resolution to certain kinds of human problems evades us. As Einstein said, "it is easier to denature plutonium than it is to denature the evil spirit of man." Corruption is a problem of the human heart. Spiritual problems require spiritual solutions. But what is the source of help?

A Changed World

The foretelling of Jesus' birth through the prophet Isaiah is well known: "For unto us a child is born, unto us a son is given: and the government shall be upon his shoulder: and his name shall be called Wonderful, Counsellor, The mighty God, The everlasting Father, The Prince of Peace" (Isaiah 9:6, King James Version). George Frideric Handel used this text in his famous oratorio *Messiah*. What he did not include was the rest of the statement: "Of the increase of his government and peace there shall be no end, upon the throne of David, and upon his kingdom, to order it, and to establish it with judgment and with justice from henceforth even for ever. The zeal of the Lord of hosts will perform this" (verse 7). This speaks of a time of Christ's rulership on earth at a yet future date. This kind of government was never part of Jesus' role in the first century. What is described here is a coming time of universal peace and justice under His care—"for law will proceed from Me, and I will make My justice rest as a light of the peoples" (Isaiah 51:4).

In a radically changed world, food and water security will be a byproduct of godly government, justice, equity and right human action. Water will be made available where needed: "The poor and needy seek water, but there is none. Their tongues fail for thirst. I, the LORD, will hear them; I, the God of Israel, will not forsake them. I will open rivers in desolate heights, and fountains in the midst of the valleys; I will make the wilderness a pool of water, and the dry land springs of water" (Isaiah 41:17–18). Right agricultural practice will lead to the blessing of abundance: "'Behold, the days are coming,' says the LORD, 'when the plowman shall overtake the reaper, and the treader of grapes him who sows seed; the mountains shall drip with sweet wine, and all the hills shall flow with it'" (Amos 9:13). This is reminiscent of the earlier promise made for obedience to God's way: "If you walk in My statutes and keep My commandments, and perform them, then I will give you rain in its season, the land shall yield its produce, and the trees of the field shall yield their fruit. Your threshing shall last till the time of vintage, and the vintage shall last till the time of sowing; you shall eat your bread to the full, and dwell in your land safely" (Leviticus 26:3–5).

The answer to the pervasive problems of the human spirit will also come as a gift from God, like food and water: "For I will pour water on him who is thirsty, and floods on the dry ground; I will pour My Spirit on your descendants, and My blessing on your offspring" (Isaiah 44:3). The prophet Jeremiah recorded God's words concerning the answer to human nature in complementary terms: "I will put My law in their minds, and write it on their hearts" (Jeremiah 31:33b). This is the way of transformation, and it alone can lead to the resolution of all human problems.

SELECTED REFERENCES:

1 International Water Management Institute, "Water for Food, Water for Life: A Comprehensive Assessment of Water Management in Agriculture" (2007).

2 Lesotho Highlands Water Project, http://www.ipocafrica.org/index. php?option=com_content&view=article&id=71&Itemid=66 (2011).

3 Peter Rogers and Susan Leal, *Running Out of Water: The Looming Crisis and Solutions to Conserve Our Most Precious Resource* (2010).

4 UN Food and Agriculture Organization, "Hunger," http://www.fao. org/hunger/en/ (2011).

5 UN Food and Water Organization, "Coping With Water Scarcity: Challenge of the Twenty-First Century" (2007).

6 Water Integrity Network, "Annual Report 2009: From Global Advocacy to Local Action" (2010).

7 The World Bank, Poverty Reduction & Equity Group, "Food Price Watch" (February 2011).

8 World Economic Forum, "Global Risks 2011, Sixth Edition" (January 2011).

RELATED ARTICLES AT WWW.VISION.ORG:

"What the Hungry Need": An interview with Ambassador Tony Hall

"Relating to Water" (Book review: *The Big Thirst: The Secret Life and Turbulent Future of Water*)

RELATED LINKS:

UN Food and Agriculture Organization: Hunger
http://www.fao.org/hunger/en/

The Food and Agriculture Organization of the United Nations (FAO), founded in 1945, maintains this informative Web site. Using graphs, tables, charts, interactive maps and more, the organization lays out the problem of world hunger in terms that just about anyone will find accessible. Included are downloadable PDF files and numerous links to additional material. Under Frequently Asked Questions, the FAO addresses such queries as "What is chronic hunger?" and "How can hunger be reduced?"

World Food Programme
http://www.wfp.org/

The World Food Programme (WFP), which bills itself as "the world's largest humanitarian agency fighting hunger worldwide," is another member of the United Nations family of organizations. On this site you'll find the complete list of the UN's Millennium Development Goals as well as detailed descriptions of the WFP fight against malnutrition and hunger in each of more than 70 countries around the world. For each nation, the site provides a map and photos, as well as a detailed overview of the current situation, an account of WFP projects and local operations, and more.

Let Justice Be Done

It's an undeniable fact that this world is filled with injustices of every conceivable kind. From ethnic cleansing to wrongful conviction and imprisonment, from theft of retirement funds to the disadvantaging of the poor, from corruption and failing government to female genital mutilation and child soldiers—the list is long, and injustice touches everyone at some point in life.

Who has not known of or experienced unfair treatment? Take the 17 people who served time on death row in the United States and are now free thanks to the advent of DNA testing. According to the New York–based Innocence Project, these 17 are among more than 297 people in 36 U.S. states who have been liberated in this way after years of wrongful imprisonment. With such releases we might conclude that justice has finally been done. But has it? What about financial compensation, or years of lost opportunity, or broken marriages and families, or never-to-be-regained reputations? What about overly ambitious lawyers and compromised judges? Is there any legal system that is 100 percent impartial?

Then there is the injustice of the death of the innocent. The Nazi bombing of Britain brought death to tens of thousands of civilians between September 1940 and May 1941—at least half of them in London. The well-known 1945 Allied firebombing of the German city of Dresden killed between 16,000 and 25,000 civilians—men, women and children. Later that year the pleas of scientists, including Albert Einstein, to spare innocent Japanese civilians went unheeded, and the United States unleashed two atomic weapons that brought about the deaths of at least 90,000 in Hiroshima and 60,000 in Nagasaki. Of course, these numbers represent but a small fragment of all the innocent deaths of the past century.

Jonathan Glover's *Humanity: A Moral History of the 20th Century* is a chronicle of some of the worst injustices. In the publisher's words, it deals with "the psychology that made possible Hiroshima, the Nazi genocide, the Gulag, the Chinese Cultural Revolution, Pol Pot's Cambodia, Rwanda, Bosnia and many other atrocities." The psychology, of course, is what we cannot easily escape, because it is fundamental to human beings. Still, Glover is not pessimistic or despairing, though he believes that "we need to look hard and clearly at some monsters inside us. But this is part of the project of caging and taming them."

This is certainly the beginning of a way ahead, but can we really do it alone? Do we have the resources within us?

Good Intentions

Justice is about fairness, equitable treatment, impartiality, objectivity, rights; the English term is rooted in the Latin *justitia* from *jus,* meaning "law" or "right." Underlying fairness and equity is the moral obligation to do what is right. Judicial systems have tried to develop means of ensuring fair treatment and imposing appropriate penalties on those proven to have done wrong by abusing others. What such systems have never been able to eradicate is human error, corruption or the downward pull of human nature. Despite best intentions, injustice remains possible in all our attempts at fairness.

We all want perfect justice, but who can deliver it continuously everywhere in the world?

The World Economic Forum's "Global Risks 2011" report lists many areas of critical concern for the next decade. They are arranged under the following three clusters: macro-economic imbalances; illegal economy; and water, food and energy.

Though the report does not make the point directly, injustice is a factor within each of these areas because of ever-present human nature. At the macro-economic level, fairness is challenged by fiscal crises, where asset price collapse, global imbalances and currency volatility are interconnected components that create a nexus of inseparable issues. Experience teaches that under severe economic pressure, nations act first by taking self-protective measures, despite modern-day efforts to promote international cooperation and the interests of the global community. Just like individuals, national entities are motivated primarily by the instinct of self-preservation.

The illegal-economy nexus is bound up in what is morally wrong, where injustice is a given. Corruption, evidenced by organized crime and illicit trade, is a significant element in the developing world. What should not be glossed over, however, is the role of demand from the developed world. This nexus of activities further contributes to the instability of fragile states, to terrorism and to geopolitical conflict. Some of the categories in the illegal sector include counterfeit pharmaceuticals and electronics, prostitution, human trafficking, and illicit drugs. The value of the illegal economy is thought to be 7–10 percent of the global economy (the "Global Risks 2011" estimate for 2009 was US$1.3 trillion and growing).

Injustice is easily triggered in the third cluster of global concerns. Selfish responses to the challenge of climate change impact not only the global environment but also energy price volatility and food and water security. As a result, issues of equity and fairness become apparent in resource wars, commodity price gouging, and irresponsible energy practices, among other outcomes. In a previous chapter, "What Shall We Eat and Drink?" we focused on the human security needs of food and water. The most obvious inequities concern the disparities between developing and developed world. In the former, a billion people go hungry every day; in the latter, 40–50 percent of all food is never eaten. About 40 percent of the world's population has no immediate access to clean water or in many cases must walk a kilometer or more to carry back supplies. For a family of five to acquire 20 liters or just over 5 U.S. gallons per person— the amount established as a minimum daily norm—would mean carrying 100 kilos (220 lbs) of water every day. At the other extreme, those with ready access flush 70 liters (18.5 U.S. gallons) down the toilet per person per day, according to an exhaustive study on residential water use undertaken by the American Water Works Research Foundation in 1999.

Attempts to resolve some of the world's human rights injustices have been the focus of the United Nations and its agencies. There has been much progress. As early as 1948, the organization formulated the Universal Declaration of Human Rights. It has proven to be the blueprint for much success in fighting inequity. More recently, however, globalized economic disruption and the failure of global governance efforts to resolve trade standoffs and environmental concerns have set progress back. The worldwide economic crisis, sparked by greed and unjust business practices, has also slowed efforts to provide adequate water and food to the disadvantaged. The standstill on trade agreements between the developed and the developing world, notably the collapse of the Doha Round of talks in 2008, has added misery to misery for the poor. Climate talks aimed at creating global norms for environmental care are logjammed as nations pursue self-interest. The 2009 Copenhagen meetings ended with what must be considered a weak statement. Lack of fairness in dealing with our common environment will punish this and future generations as concerns food, water and energy.

Reluctantly we have to admit that while there has been great improvement in some respects, injustice remains embedded in human life. According to the 2010 annual report of the International Commission of Jurists, "despite the fact that 160 States are parties to the International Covenant on Economic, Social and Cultural Rights (ICESCR), and should therefore have incorporated its provisions into domestic law and provide[d] judicial remedies to individuals alleging a violation of their rights, *victims continue to face tremendous difficulties in accessing justice*" (emphasis added).

"Justice Is Far From Us"

In the first century, the state of the world caused one man to reflect that justice was nowhere to be found and that no one was "righteous." Writing a letter to the congregations in Rome, the apostle Paul based his conclusion in part on the Hebrew prophet Isaiah's words: "The way of peace they have not known, and there is no justice in their ways; they have made themselves crooked paths; whoever takes that way shall not know peace" (Isaiah 59:8; see also Romans 3:15–17). Paul lived in the Graeco-Roman world; Isaiah lived centuries earlier in the kingdom of Judah. Separated by 700 years, they expressed the same conclusion about humanity. A major theme in Isaiah's writing is the need for justice to be established.

Early in his book, the prophet describes a corrupt society where people act "to rob the needy of justice, and to take what is right from the poor of My people, that widows may be their prey, and that they may rob the fatherless" (Isaiah 10:2). Around the same period another prophet to Judah, Habbakuk, wrote about the effects of the failure to practice right behavior toward neighbor: "Therefore the law is powerless, and justice never goes forth. For the wicked surround the righteous; therefore perverse judgment proceeds" (Habakkuk 1:4). This is surely an observation that resonates with anyone who has experienced unjust treatment at the hands of those best equipped to help.

No doubt Paul would have found both these passages accurate descriptions for his time too. One of his contemporaries certainly did. Writing of unjust employers, Jesus' brother James says, "Indeed the wages of the laborers who mowed your fields, which you kept back by fraud, cry out; and the cries of the reapers have reached the ears of the Lord of Sabaoth. You have lived on the earth in pleasure and luxury" (James 5:4–5).

The social disorder that results from injustice is reflected in Isaiah's further words (he could be writing of the 21st century): "Therefore justice is far from us, nor does righteousness overtake us; we look for light, but there is darkness! For brightness, but we walk in blackness! . . . Justice is turned back, and righteousness stands afar off; for truth is fallen in the street, and equity cannot enter" (Isaiah 59:9, 14). The person who recognizes what has happened and holds on to right values puts himself in great danger: "so truth fails, and he who departs from evil makes himself a prey" (verse 15).

Societies have such problems because justice and righteousness (right thinking and living) are not natural to the human sphere. But these godly characteristics may be practiced individually now and will ultimately become the basis of all society. Injustice will give way to justice when righteousness becomes the standard for all behavior. Isaiah knew this well. Speaking of a future godly global ruler, he said, "Of the increase of His government and peace there will be no end, upon the throne of David and over His kingdom, to order it and establish it with judgment and justice, from that time forward, even forever. The zeal of the LORD of hosts will perform this" (Isaiah 9:7; see also 16:5).

This is understood to be a reference to the coming of the Messiah. Yet Christ did not fulfill these aspects of His prophesied role when He came in the first century. This is for a future time when universal justice will become reality. As Matthew's Gospel quotes the Father's words about Jesus: "Behold! My servant whom I have chosen, My Beloved in whom My soul is well pleased! I will put My Spirit upon Him, and He will declare justice to the Gentiles [the nations]" (Matthew 12:18). This, too, is from Isaiah, where the prophet shows that the Messiah will be persistent in His pursuit of fairness and equity for all: "He will not fail nor be discouraged, till He has established justice in the earth; and the coastlands shall wait for His law" (Isaiah 42:4).

We all want perfect justice, but who can deliver it continuously everywhere in the world? This is the only One.

SELECTED REFERENCES:

1 AWWA Research Foundation and American Water Works Association, *Residential End Uses of Water* (1999).

2 Charles Fishman, *The Big Thirst: The Secret Life and Turbulent Future of Water* (2011).

3 Jonathan Glover, *Humanity: A Moral History of the Twentieth Century* (1999).

4 International Commission of Jurists, "Annual Report 2010: Protecting Human Rights and Advancing the Rule of Law" (April 2011).

5 United Nations Development Programme, *Human Development Report 2006*, "Beyond Scarcity: Power, Poverty and the Global Water Crisis" (2006).

6 World Economic Forum, "Global Risks 2011," 6th ed. (January 2011).

RELATED ARTICLES AT WWW.VISION.ORG:

"Taming the Monster Inside Us": An interview with Jonathan Glover

Sidebar: "Human Rights"

Sidebar: "Justice and Righteousness"

Sidebar: "What Can We Do Now?"

Hot Evil, Cold Evil

Have you ever heard of hot and cold evil?

A number of years ago a friend introduced me to the concept. Hot evil, he said, was the kind that outraged most people immediately. Examples might be a violent crime against innocent children, or an attempt at genocide. Cold evil was far more insidious—the kind of evil that many of us have participated in through apathy or seeming powerlessness. What Adolf Hitler did to the Jewish people and other minorities was hot evil. Those who were aware of that atrocity and participated in it by doing nothing took part in cold evil.

Was the one evil worse than the other? Surely they were both horrible. Of course, the perpetrator of evil is reckoned worse because of direct involvement. But as Edmund Burke said, the only thing necessary for the triumph of evil is for good men to do nothing. So the so-called powerless can be implicated very seriously.

It's a familiar thought, and one echoed in a statement from American political philosopher Hannah Arendt. She once wrote about Adolf Eichmann, who was convicted of horrific war crimes against the Jewish people. She said, "The trouble with Eichmann was precisely that so many were like him, and that the many were neither perverted nor sadistic, that they were, and still are, terribly and terrifyingly normal. From the viewpoint of our legal institutions and of our moral standards of judgment, this normality was much more terrifying than all the atrocities put together."

So which is worse, hot evil or cold evil? Does it even make sense to choose between one evil and another? The point we so easily forget is that in choosing between two evils, whichever choice we make, *both* are still evil. The problem here, as Hannah Arendt pointed out, is that ordinary human nature can lead to some pretty awful behavior.

How many times have we regretted doing nothing and allowing another to suffer the impact of evil intentions? Are we our brother's keeper? That famous phrase comes from one of the most ancient accounts in Western culture. It's the timeless story of Cain and Abel. What happened to those two brothers is a powerful warning of what can happen when hot evil is not mastered on an individual level.

The account of their fateful encounter is in the book of Genesis, chapter 4. It's a primal account of the way human nature can take any of us when unrestrained.

When you read the account of the two brothers, the difference in attitude is apparent. Genesis says: "Now Abel was a keeper of sheep, but Cain was a tiller of the ground. And in the process of time it came to pass that Cain brought an offering of the fruit of the ground to the LORD. Abel also brought of the firstborn of his flock and of their fat. And the LORD respected Abel and his offering, but He did not respect Cain and his offering. And Cain was very angry, and his countenance fell. So the LORD said to Cain, 'Why are you angry? And why has your countenance fallen? If you do well, will you not be accepted? And if you do not do well, sin lies at the door. And its desire is for you, but you should rule over it.' Now Cain talked with Abel his brother; and it came to pass, when they were in the field, that Cain rose up against Abel his brother and killed him" (verses 2b–8).

Abel was doing the right thing, but Cain was not. He allowed his obsessional hatred to drive him on. He failed to master it. Cain, in fact, was obsessed with his brother's right behavior, and his own inadequacy became a source of Cain's animosity. The *Bible Knowledge Commentary* puts it this way: "It is as if he could not wait to destroy his brother—a natural man's solution to his own failure."

In Genesis the account continues: "Then the LORD said to Cain, 'Where is Abel your brother?' He said, 'I do not know. Am I my brother's keeper?' And He said, 'What have you done? The voice of your brother's blood cries out to Me from the ground'" (verses 9–10).

What is the source of this kind of behavior? The apostle John makes the answer clear in one of his letters to the early Christian Church. He says in reference to Cain and Abel: "In this the children of God and the children of the devil are manifest: Whoever does not practice righteousness is not of God, nor is he who does not love his brother. For this is the message that you heard from the beginning, that we should love one another, not as Cain who was of the wicked one and murdered his brother. And why did he murder him? Because his works were evil and his brother's righteous" (1 John 3:10–12).

So the antidote for hot evil lies in the mastery of sin and in the individual overthrow of the power of the ultimate malevolent force. And what about cold evil? The account of Cain and Abel also hints at the concern we must express for each other in the concept of being our brother's keeper.

Are we our brother's keeper? Yes, indeed we are. Are we subject to wrong influences and impulses? Yes, we are. Is there a way out? Yes, there is. The answer lies in changing human nature. And that sounds impossible. But is it? We'll discuss that next.

Changing
Human Nature

The role that envy, jealousy and anger played in the Bible's first murder is most instructive. When Cain killed Abel, he set a pattern that has become all too familiar. His obsession with his brother's goodness in the face of his own failure to do right brought him to the point of murder.

Human nature has obsessive tendencies. It has proven very difficult to master. According to writer Henry Miller, "man has demonstrated that he is master of everything— except his own nature." Albert Einstein claimed that it was easier to denature plutonium than to change human nature.

So how do we overcome our nature? God told Cain that sin was crouching at his door, in waiting for him. Cain was supposed to master the impulse to do wrong. How could he have done that?

The answer comes in the writings of a man who struggled with his nature more than most. Listen to these words. Do they describe your frustrations with yourself? "For what I will to do, that I do not practice; but what I hate, that I do. If, then, I do what I will not to do, I agree with the law that it is good. But now, it is no longer I who do it, but sin that dwells in me. For I know that in me (that is, in my flesh) nothing good dwells; for to will is present with me, but how to perform what is good I do not find. For the good that I will to do, I do not do; but the evil I will not to do, that I practice" (Romans 7:15b–19).

It's a description of a man caught up in his human weaknesses—someone who was trying to live the right way. The apostle Paul recognized that without outside help he could do nothing—that human nature is, as he said, antagonistic to the laws and ways of God.

He wrote in his letter to the early Christians at Rome that "to be carnally minded is death, but to be spiritually minded is life and peace. Because the carnal mind is enmity against God; for it is not subject to the law of God, nor indeed can be" (Romans 8:6–7).

What did he mean by "the carnal mind"? The carnal mind is the natural human mind. It is a mind that of itself would never submit to the law of God over it. In other words, of ourselves, we are unwilling to have God rule over us. The human mind has to be changed by God's intervention. Then it becomes possible for the Spirit of God to enlighten us and to show us what we really are capable of—both good and bad.

Paul came to see that with the Spirit of God at work in us the requirement of the law of God could be met. Without His Spirit we can never overcome our nature.

At the beginning of the New Testament Church the disciples found themselves in a very public exchange with their fellow citizens—those who had participated in the death of Christ. Their countrymen were cut to the heart when they realized that they had participated in the murder of an innocent man. Notice how the book of Acts describes their reaction. In response to the disciples, they said: "'Men and brethren, what shall we do?' Then Peter said to them,

'Repent, and let every one of you be baptized in the name of Jesus Christ for the remission of sins; and you shall receive the gift of the Holy Spirit. For the promise is to you and to your children, and to all who are afar off, as many as the Lord our God will call'" (Acts 2:37–39).

God's forgiveness can come only when there is genuine repentance—a turning and going in the opposite direction. When humans make that commitment to change at a deep level, then it is possible to start keeping the law of God in its original spiritual intent.

Missing the Mark

At a time when many of us are perplexed by the mounting evidence of evil at work in the world, a respected commentator on religious matters has come forward to assure us that we need not be so concerned. I was stunned by a recent contribution to BBC Radio's *Thought for the Day* by author and theologian Martin Palmer. This latest effort to achieve relevance by turning to humanist and other philosophical concepts has allowed the broadcasting of ideas that are dangerous and destructive to human life. Perhaps I should not have been so shocked, but it was one of the most blatant attempts yet to blur the distinction between good and evil. It is reminiscent of Satan's own attempt in the Garden of Eden to get Eve to accept his way of thinking as superior to God's. The Bible tells us that Satan did persuade her and in turn her husband, Adam, to believe that the tree of the knowledge of good and evil was a better source of insight and discernment than was the tree of life.

Palmer has written several books on the history of religion. Perhaps it is this background that led him to claim that "[the] notion of a world of good and evil was developed in Iran by a man called Mani, who was born almost exactly 1,800 years ago. [He] believed that the world was a battleground for a cosmic struggle between the absolute force for Good—God—and the absolute force for Evil—Satan. . . . Mani helped define the idea that difference was threatening and evil, rather than simply part of the way things are."

Telling us that good and evil is a distinction that came late in human history and that it is just one man's opinion is playing fast and loose with thousands of years of world history prior to Mani, when people did know that good and evil existed. It is to claim that there really is no such thing as sin. Palmer compounds his error and even misappropriates God's Word to support his case when he says: "But we didn't always think like this, nor do we need to. . . . There is and always has been an alternative to the good-versus-evil worldview. If what we believe and do is true to our own understandings, then there is, actually, no need to think that different beliefs or lifestyles are therefore necessarily wrong or evil. Or as the prophet Micah puts it, 'What does God require of you, but to be just, to love kindness, and to walk humbly with *your* understanding of God.'"

This quote from Micah omits its important first clause, "He has shown you, O man, what is good" (Micah 6:8). So the prophet did recognize that "good" is a godly concept. But more troubling is Palmer's insertion of the words "understanding of" to suggest that Micah accepted various equivalent understandings of God. The prophet did not say that. Furthermore, he would have known that when God presented our first parents with the two trees and instructed them regarding which would give them life and which would lead to death, God drew a distinction in the clearest of terms.

Knowing the difference between good and evil is one of the most important pieces of understanding we can have. The Scriptures are consistent in showing us the difference from one end of the Bible to the other—and all predating Mani, the Iranian mystic. The prophet Isaiah had issued God's warning to the morally ambivalent 900 years earlier:

"Woe to those who call evil good, and good evil; who put darkness for light, and light for darkness; who put bitter for sweet, and sweet for bitter!" (Isaiah 5:20). And thankfully, about 150 years before Mani, the apostle John advised: "Beloved, do not imitate what is evil, but what is good. He who does good is of God, but he who does evil has not seen God" (3 John 11).

Why Suffering?

Throughout history people have asked why, if God is both good and all-powerful, He doesn't intercede to prevent pain and suffering in the world. Is there an answer?

How many people have turned away from belief in God because of suffering? One for sure was the Nobel Prize–winning author of many 20th-century works, Samuel Beckett. According to his official biographer, James Knowlson, "it was on the key issue of pain, suffering and death that Beckett's religious faith faltered and quickly foundered." In the 1920s the streets of his hometown, Dublin, were filled with men who had returned from the Great War, shell-shocked, gassed, maimed or dismembered. The confrontation with reality clashed with Beckett's comfortable upper-middle-class background.

By his own admission, another incident in his student days contributed to the rejection of God and Christianity. Raised as an Anglican, Beckett attended church services with his father one Sunday evening to hear a family friend preach. Canon Dobbs spoke about his visits to "the sick, the suffering, the dying and the bereaved." His way of consoling people in such straits was to tell them, "[Christ's] crucifixion was only the beginning. You must contribute to the kitty." Beckett was appalled at the failure to explain undeserved suffering and the attempted rationale for a growing mountain of pain. To say that suffering somehow prepared one for a better afterlife made no sense to him either; he considered it an affront to the sufferer.

In 1954 Beckett spent three and a half months with his brother Frank, who was dying of lung cancer. According to Knowlson, the experience was harrowing, the passage of time endless, the grief acute, the depression profound. Sam's pain was matched only by his feelings following the death of his father in 1933 and his mother in 1950. As he had waited for his mother to die from complications of Parkinson's and a broken femur, "he [had] thought with bitter irony of his own situation, an agnostic who desperately needed God to blame for the unnecessary nature of his mother's suffering."

Most of Beckett's work is dark and pessimistic, centered on the futility and hopelessness of human life. His highly influential play, *Waiting for Godot* (1952), is the tale of two men who wait for the arrival of someone who never comes and will never come. Thought by many to emphasize that belief in God does nothing but disappoint in an otherwise meaningless existence, the play is nevertheless rich in biblical allusions (the tree of life, Adam, Cain and Abel, the crucifixion, the two thieves, repentance, prayer). Some have also seen parallels between it and the book of Job.

Despite his agnosticism, Beckett wrote with a Bible and concordances at hand, as biographer Anthony Cronin notes. But Beckett's access to the Scriptures did not reveal to him its truths about suffering in this life. Instead he remarked to writer-director Colin Duckworth, "Christianity is a mythology with which I am perfectly familiar. So naturally I use it"—often in ironic and sarcastic ways, Cronin adds.

According to Mary Bryden, professor at the University of Reading and former president of the Samuel Beckett Society, "the hypothesised God who emerges from Beckett's texts is one who is both cursed for his perverse absence and cursed for his surveillant presence. He is by turns dismissed, satirised, or ignored, but he, and his tortured son, are never definitively discarded."

Similar Plot, Different Ending

Another renowned 20th-century writer, C.S. Lewis, was born a few years earlier and a few miles farther north in Belfast. He, too, began life an Anglican in an upper-middle-class home, losing his mother to cancer as a child. After rejecting Christianity as a 15-year-old and becoming an atheist, Lewis, aged 32 and now a professor of English at Oxford, returned to the faith of his upbringing partly through the influence of his Roman Catholic colleague, J.R.R. Tolkien. As a result, his writings became focused on Christian themes, and he became one of the religion's best-known apologists. His collected novels, *The Space Trilogy* and *The Chronicles of Narnia*, contain many Christian allusions.

Though he had seen death and dying firsthand in trench warfare in France and been wounded by friendly fire, Lewis came to a very different conclusion about suffering than Beckett did. In 1940 he wrote *The Problem of Pain* and in 1961, following great personal loss and an intense struggle with his belief, the initially pseudonymous *A Grief Observed*. Friends actually recommended the latter book to him as a help in his grieving, not realizing that he was its author. Only after his death was it republished under his own name.

After many years as a bachelor, Lewis had met and married the American Jewish writer Helen Joy Gresham (nee Davidman), who had been drawn away from atheism and convinced of Christianity by Lewis's writings. Their marriage in 1957 came only after she had been diagnosed with bone cancer. After remission and then relapse, she died a painful death in 1960. That he had loved so much and lost so much in so short a time caused Lewis to question God's goodness.

In *The Problem of Pain* he wrote, "The problem of reconciling human suffering with the existence of a God who loves, is only insoluble so long as we attach a trivial meaning to the word 'love', and look on things as if man were the centre of them. Man is not the centre. God does not exist for the sake of man. Man does not exist for his own sake. 'Thou hast created all things, and for thy pleasure they are and were created.'" Later in the book he wrote, "I am not arguing that pain is not painful. Pain hurts. That is what the word means. I am only trying to show that the old Christian doctrine of being made 'perfect through suffering' is not incredible. To prove it palatable is beyond my design."

In *A Grief Observed*, which is based on notebooks he kept as he tried to cope with his wife's death, he struggles with the reality of the experience of loss rather than returning to the intellectual arguments he had put forward earlier. He is at times at a complete impasse, angry and doubting God's goodness, feeling that God is behind a door with all the bolts fastened.

But toward the end of the book, he writes, "When I lay these questions before God I get no answer. But a rather special sort of 'No answer.' It is not the locked door. It is more like a silent, certainly not uncompassionate, gaze. As though He shook His head not in refusal but waiving the question. Like, 'Peace, child; you don't understand.'

"Can a mortal ask questions which God finds unanswerable? Quite easily, I should think. All nonsense questions are unanswerable. How many hours are there in a mile? Is yellow square or round? Probably half the questions we ask—half our great theological and metaphysical problems—are like that."

The book concludes with a quote from Dante's *Paradiso*, or "Heaven." Introducing it, Lewis writes, "[Joy] said not to me but to the chaplain, 'I am at peace with God.' She smiled, but not at me. *Poi si tornò all' eterna fontana*" ("Then she turned to the eternal fountain"; i.e., God).

The Problem of Evil

What both Beckett and Lewis struggled with in their own way was a problem that has troubled most people at some point, including other notables such as Mark Twain and Charles Darwin. It is the dilemma known as theodicy, literally the justice of God or the justification of God, or better still, justifying God's behavior as far as the presence of evil in His creation is concerned. How can a good Creator God exist alongside evil or suffering in the world? German philosopher Gottfried Leibniz coined the word in 1710 as he tried to demonstrate that God's goodness is not incompatible with the presence of evil. It was his attempt to answer the writing of a skeptic, Pierre Bayle, who said that suffering proves that God is not good and not all-powerful. This is, of course, a standard argument used by skeptics to bolster agnosticism and atheism.

Often in these kinds of discussions you have the feeling that the humans asking the questions are seeing only a small piece of the picture. As Lewis says, there are nonsense questions. Is it possible that the contradiction posed in the theodicy debate is a red herring in the first place and should not be considered, because it is a nonsense question? Could it be that once God's plan and purpose are discovered, then suffering, though never easy or something we prefer, becomes explainable?

One of the pieces of the puzzle is to understand that before humans came on the scene, there was a realm into which spirit beings introduced evil. According to the Hebrew Scriptures, it was an otherwise perfect environment, until Satan (the Adversary) and his followers opposed God. The prophet Ezekiel describes this being, before he became the archenemy, in these terms:

"You were the seal of perfection, full of wisdom and perfect in beauty. You were in Eden, the garden of God. . . . You were the anointed cherub who covers; I established you; you were on the holy mountain of God; you walked back and forth in the midst of fiery stones. You were perfect in your ways from the day you were created" (Ezekiel 28:12–15a).

But then there came a point where a wrong, competitive attitude entered him. He allowed himself the luxury of an imagined alternative, where he and not God would be in command. Thus sin "was found in you" (verse 15b). Violence against God and His way became his modus operandi: "By the abundance of your trading you became filled with violence within, and you sinned; therefore I cast you as a profane thing out of the mountain of God; and I destroyed you, O covering cherub, from the midst of the fiery stones" (verse 16).

This state of mind resulted in a war against God that drew in one third of the angels (see Isaiah 14:12–14; Revelation 12:3–4). It was a possibility because God had created spirit beings with free choice.

So when humans came along there was already evil in the universe and thus the possibility of sin and suffering for humanity, if they chose to follow the lead of Satan. And choose they could, because God also created *them* with free moral agency. They could decide to follow God's way or reject it. If they did that they would be in a position of deciding for themselves what is right and wrong. Early in the story of humanity, we read that human beings chose to proceed without God. This alone is a cause of the effect that we call suffering.

The apostle Paul understood the connection between those early actions and continuing society. Sometimes we suffer because of what others before us have done: "Just as through one man sin entered the world, and death through sin, and thus death spread to all men, because all sinned" (Romans 5:12).

It is clear that God expected humans to choose to do the right thing even after Adam and Eve rejected Him and He expelled them from the Garden. To their son, Cain, He said, "Why are you angry? And why has your countenance fallen? If you do well, will you not be accepted? And if you do not do well, sin lies at the door. And its desire is for you, but you should rule over it" (Genesis 4:6–7). That is, like Adam and Eve, Cain could have made the right choice and not suffered one of the consequences of sin, which is suffering.

Part of God's great purpose is to help humanity see what the price of going the wrong way really is—how costly it is. That cannot be learned if every time the consequence is about to play out, He intervenes to stop it, so that there is no evident connection between sin and consequence. If humans choose to go the wrong way, the only way they can learn to choose right is to become aware of the result of wrongdoing.

Without this kind of background knowledge, our attempts to understand and explain evil or suffering in a world created by a good God is like entering a movie two-thirds of the way through and expecting to understand the plot. What happens then is that we ask nonsense questions. Evil is simply not something that flows from God.

The Wrong Question

One of the complaints that agnostics and atheists make is that God does not intervene to *prevent* evil consequences for humans. Yet if He did restrain humans from acting at every wrong turn, they would soon resent his taking away their freedom to act as they choose. The fact of free moral agency within a gradually unfolding plan is one of the reasons God does not automatically intervene to prevent epidemics or road accidents or abuse or wars.

So rather than complaining about God's lack of intervention, it would be better to adopt a humble approach and start with the fact that there is probably something we don't understand from our human vantage point. It is the kind of attitude spoken of in the book of Isaiah—because whatever it is that God is doing in the world, whatever His plan is, our response to it ought to be based on the following: "Surely you have things turned around! Shall the potter be esteemed as the clay; for shall the thing made say of him who made it, 'He did not make me'? Or shall the thing formed say of him who formed it, 'He has no understanding'?" (Isaiah 29:16).

"You have things turned around!" That's to say, you are asking the wrong question. Should you be questioning God as Creator? Should you be denying Him? Isaiah continues the thought later when he says, "Woe to him who strives with his Maker! Let the potsherd strive with the potsherds of the earth! Shall the clay say to him who forms it, 'What are you making?' Or shall your handiwork say, 'He has no hands'?" (Isaiah 45:9).

The point here is that right perspective and humility are necessary to begin to get located in the right relationship with God. Humans are mostly dislocated. They don't know where they are in terms of God. They don't understand Him or know His purpose. No wonder, then, that so many come to wrong conclusions about life and about Him.

Job was a righteous man, yet he was not rightly located with respect to God. He was a blameless and upright man, but his understanding was incomplete. God allowed him to be tested by the archenemy, a factor in some suffering, in order to bring him to a much better place spiritually (see Job 1:6–12).

By the end of the book, Job is able to listen to God as He asks dozens of questions, none of which Job can answer. He can only repent, seeing himself for what he is: "Then Job answered the LORD and said: 'I know that You can do everything, and that no purpose of Yours can be withheld from You. . . . Therefore I have uttered what I did not understand, things too wonderful for me, which I did not know. . . . I have heard of You by the hearing of the ear, but now my eye sees You. Therefore I abhor myself, and repent in dust and ashes'" (Job 42:1–6).

Now he is finally where he needs to be and can be blessed much more than before.

Paul Weighs In

In Romans 9 Paul discusses an issue that may have troubled some of his fellow Israelites: Why had God seemingly turned His back on them and begun working with gentiles? It's another facet of the theodicy debate: Is God good? Is He just?

In Paul's words: "Is there unrighteousness with God? Certainly not! For He says to Moses, 'I will have mercy on whomever I will have mercy, and I will have compassion on whomever I will have compassion.' So then it is not of him who wills, nor of him who runs, but of God who shows mercy" (Romans 9:14–16).

In this extended passage, Paul uses the same analogy of clay and potter as Isaiah recorded: "But indeed, O man, who are you to reply against God? Will the thing formed say to him who formed it, 'Why have you made me like this?' Does not the potter have power over the clay, from the same lump to make one vessel for honor and another for dishonor?" (verses 20–21).

In other words, as we are seeing, you can come in part way through the movie and not understand; you can begin to argue, complain, ask inappropriate or nonsense questions, and even become violent.

Paul was such a person at one point in his life. He had a great deal of knowledge, but to little good effect. Referring to his life as an observant Jew, he said, "I was formerly a blasphemer, a persecutor, and an insolent man; but I obtained mercy because I did it ignorantly in unbelief" (1 Timothy 1:13).

When Paul was in that condition, Luke tells us, "he made havoc of the church, entering every house, and dragging off men and women, committing them to prison" (Acts 8:3).

He thought he was right to blaspheme and be rude, arrogant and violent. He later came to see what he didn't understand at the time. But God allowed the suffering he caused. And some of the people who suffered were God's followers.

Paul later wrote about his personal suffering, which sometimes came from the kind of persecution he himself had engaged in formerly: "From the Jews five times I received forty stripes minus one. Three times I was beaten with rods; once I was stoned; three times I was shipwrecked; a night and a day I have been in the deep; in journeys often, in perils of waters, in perils of robbers, in perils of my own countrymen, in perils of the Gentiles, in perils in the city, in perils in the wilderness, in perils in the sea, in perils among false brethren; in weariness and toil, in sleeplessness often, in hunger and thirst, in fastings often, in cold and nakedness—besides the other things, what comes upon me daily: my deep concern for all the churches" (2 Corinthians 11:24–28).

On other occasions he suffered because God chose not to help him, so that a greater good might come of his difficulties: "A thorn in the flesh was given to me, a messenger of Satan to buffet me, lest I be exalted above measure. Concerning this thing I pleaded with the Lord three times that it might depart from me. And He said to me, 'My grace is sufficient for you, for My strength is made perfect in weakness.' . . . Therefore I take pleasure in infirmities, in reproaches, in needs, in persecutions, in distresses, for Christ's sake. For when I am weak, then I am strong" (2 Corinthians 12:7–10).

One of the concepts that Samuel Beckett could not accept in his student days was what Paul seems to refer to in Colossians 1:24: "I now rejoice in my sufferings for you, and fill up in my flesh what is lacking in the afflictions of Christ, for the sake of His body, which is the church."

This is a difficult verse, especially as translated from the Greek. One of the most satisfying explanations is that "afflictions of Christ" is not a reference to His final sufferings but to the woes, or tribulations, that will precede His coming (see Revelation 8:13). Paul saw his suffering for the Church as making a contribution to these woes so that Christ would come. The phrase "afflictions of Christ" appears nowhere in reference to His crucifixion. Further, His sufferings cannot be incomplete.

If this is true, then Beckett based his rejection of belief in part on a misunderstanding, passed on by his family's friend, Canon Dobbs.

Paul provides clearer understanding of the relationship between Christ's sufferings and the believer's own when he writes: ". . . I have suffered the loss of all things, and count them as rubbish, that I may gain Christ and be found in Him, . . . that I may know Him and the power of His resurrection, and the fellowship of His sufferings, being conformed to His death, if, by any means, I may attain to the resurrection from the dead" (Philippians 3:8–11).

Perfection Through Suffering

We noted earlier a reference to Christ's suffering in C.S. Lewis's writings. He said, "I am only trying to show that the old Christian doctrine of being made 'perfect through suffering' is not incredible."

This is a reference to Hebrews 2:9–10: "But we see Jesus, who was made a little lower than the angels, for the suffering of death crowned with glory and honor, that He, by the grace of God, might taste death for everyone. For it was fitting for Him, for whom are all things and by whom are all things, in bringing many sons to glory, to make the captain of their salvation perfect through sufferings."

Here is an idea that is foreign to most if not all other religious persuasions—that we can become perfect by suffering. Yet that is what God ordained for His own Son.

Our natural inclination is to say, "Don't talk to me about suffering. I don't want to face it. I don't want to suffer." This is an absolutely normal human reaction.

It was also Christ's reaction in Gethsemane just before the crucifixion: "He went a little farther and fell on His face, and prayed, saying, 'O My Father, if it is possible, let this cup pass from Me; nevertheless, not as I will, but as You will.' . . . Again, a second time, He went away and prayed, saying, 'O My Father, if this cup cannot pass away from Me unless I drink it, Your will be done'" (Matthew 26:39–42).

Christ had to suffer; He was made perfect through those sufferings. And His suffering included more than the immediate events leading to His death and the crucifixion itself.

The fact that Christ suffered means that He is now able to help human beings even more meaningfully. There can be a bond between us, knowing that He understands and stands ready to help: "For in that He Himself has suffered, being tempted [tested], He is able to aid those who are tempted" (Hebrews 2:18).

Coming in on the human drama part way through and being uninformed of the history to that point is no way to understand the great plan and purpose God is working out through beings made from clay, yet with free will and an awesome future. As Paul concludes, "I consider that the sufferings of this present time are not worthy to be compared with the glory which shall be revealed in us" (Romans 8:18).

This is a truth to dwell on when difficult times come.

SELECTED REFERENCES:

1 Samuel Beckett, *Waiting for Godot* (1952).

2 Mary Bryden, *Samuel Beckett and the Idea of God* (1998).

3 Anthony Cronin, *Samuel Beckett: The Last Modernist* (1997).

4 Colin Duckworth, *Angels of Darkness: Dramatic Effect in Samuel Beckett* (1972).

5 Walter Hooper, *C.S. Lewis: A Complete Guide to His Life & Works* (1996).

6 James Knowlson, *Damned to Fame: The Life of Samuel Beckett* (1996).

7 C.S. Lewis, *The Problem of Pain* (1940).

8 C.S. Lewis, *A Grief Observed* (1961).

RELATED ARTICLES AT WWW.VISION.ORG:

Sidebar: "Theodicy"

"J.R.R. Tolkien: Speaker of Footnotes"

"Mark Twain: The Whited Sepulchre"

Finding God's Forgiveness

Even religions disagree on how to define forgiveness. And the belief systems that claim the Bible as their basis have significantly divergent views on this pivotal subject. So just what does the Bible say?

Forgiveness is a growing issue in a world that's struggling with the personal impact of current and recent wars, domestic violence, theft, betrayal, deceit, abuse and murder. The list doesn't stop there, because what needs to be forgiven covers every human wrong—what the Bible terms "sin." And that troubling word is one reason to agree on terminology from the start. Without that, clarity about forgiveness and related issues from a biblical perspective will be impossible to achieve. Without a common language, the best we'll do is to talk at cross purposes.

Just what does the Bible say about sin, repentance *and* forgiveness? Who does the forgiving—God, the victim, both? What does it mean to go the other way (repent)? And what exactly is sin?

Defining sin is central to sorting out what needs to be forgiven, why, how and by whom. The early New Testament Church leaders have much to say about the subject, and the basis of their understanding is the Hebrew Scriptures and the teaching of Jesus of Nazareth. The apostle John puts it this way: "All wrongdoing is sin" (1 John 5:17, English Standard Version). The New King James translation of the New Testament Greek has "unrighteousness" for "wrongdoing." That's to say, sin is the opposite of righteousness, or counter to the way God would do things if He were here.

John also tells us that "whoever commits sin also commits lawlessness, and sin is lawlessness" (1 John 3:4). In other words, whatever is not in accord with God's established standard is outside of His law and is "wickedness," and therefore sin. The composition of that law leads to the understanding that sin flows broadly in two directions—against God and against fellow human beings. Whenever people act contrary to that law, they sin specifically against either God or fellow man, and often both. Sin, by definition, harms relationships and people.

One of the things that struck the apostle Paul so forcibly about the human condition in the Greco-Roman world of the first century was that men and women "did not like to retain God in their knowledge." The result of that damaged relationship was that God had no choice but to allow the consequences to fall into place. So, according to Paul, "God gave them over to a debased mind, to do those things which are not fitting" (Romans 1:28). The refusal to acknowledge God's existence led inevitably to a mind incapable of discerning right from wrong on God's terms and the inability to resist the pull of human nature's selfishness. The result is a list of bad actors and behaviors of the worst kind—people who practice "all unrighteousness, sexual immorality, wickedness, covetousness, maliciousness; . . . envy, murder, strife, deceit, evil-mindedness; they are whisperers, backbiters, haters of God, violent, proud, boasters, inventors of evil things, disobedient to parents, undiscerning, untrustworthy, unloving, unforgiving, unmerciful" (verses 29–31).

Here again is the breaking of law in two directions— toward God and toward man. So sin is anything that violates the law that relates to either party.

In God's system of justice, there is always a penalty to be paid for sin. Mercy can be extended, but a price will always be paid. Because every human who has lived has sinned, the penalty (eternal death) hangs over each individual until removed somehow. Unique to this biblical system (as opposed to other religious belief systems) is the death of a perfect being in a voluntary sacrificial act to pay the penalty for sin in place of the sinner. Paul explained this to the congregation at Rome, saying that "when we were still without strength, in due time Christ died for the ungodly. . . . God demonstrates His own love toward us, in that while we were still sinners, Christ died for us" (Romans 5:6, 8). The reason He died is to set humanity right, or bring reconciliation with God the Father by clearing away the death penalty and the sin that impedes a right relationship with Him. Once that is done, human beings are freed to develop the kind of relationship that leads only to beneficial results.

To Forgive Is Divine

The Bible speaks of extending forgiveness toward others and of God forgiving human beings. There is a difference between the two actions. First, what does forgiveness by God entail? How does God go about wiping the slate clean of sin?

To take one example, what does He do in the case of the persecution and murder of the innocent? Is it simply that the victim or the victim's family asks, and God grants forgiveness to the perpetrator? Is it that the guilty need do nothing?

Many take Jesus' words on the crucifixion stake, "Father, forgive them, for they do not know what they do" (Luke 23:34), as evidence that all that is needed for others to be forgiven is the request of the victim. Yet seven weeks after that horrific death, the apostle Peter told an audience of some of Christ's now-remorseful persecutors that they had *yet* to repent. That's to say, they were not forgiven. What Jesus had said did not automatically bring forgiveness. His words were more about His attitude toward His persecutors than a request that God override the need for repentance. It's clear from the account in Acts that recognition of wrongful acts and repentance are necessary for forgiveness to take place. This would include recognition of their guilt in Jesus' death and of their own lifelong sinful ways. Peter told his listeners, "Therefore let all the house of Israel know assuredly that God has made this Jesus, whom you crucified, both Lord and Christ." The account continues: "Now when they heard this, they were cut to the heart, and said to Peter and the rest of the apostles, 'Men and brethren, what shall we do?' Then Peter said to them, 'Repent, and let every one of you be baptized in the name of Jesus Christ for the remission of your sins; and you shall receive the gift of the Holy Spirit" (Acts 2:36–38).

Reconciliation to the Father is the result of accepting Christ's death in place of the sinner, the sinner's recognition of wrongdoing and of *being* wrong, and the desire to live the right way. Christ's sacrifice for sin cannot be applied in a specific sense until there is this kind of individual and genuine repentance, backed by sincere effort to go in the right direction.

Luke's Gospel includes three parables that relate to repentance (Luke 15). They picture God's joy when a person turns to living the right way. Jesus creates these stories around the concept of things lost and then found.

The first example concerns a single lost sheep that its owner goes out to recover. Once found, he returns home with it and calls his neighbors, "saying to them, 'Rejoice with me, for I have found my sheep which was lost!' I say to you that likewise there will be more joy in heaven over one sinner who repents than over ninety-nine just persons who need no repentance" (verses 6–7). Jesus links the account with delight in heaven at repentance. In other words, once again, sinners are forgiven in part through repentance.

The point is emphasized in the second example. This time it is loss of wealth in the form of money. A woman who has lost a silver coin finds it and "calls her friends and neighbors together, saying, 'Rejoice with me, for I have found the piece which I lost.' Likewise, I say to you, there is joy in the presence of the angels of God over one sinner who repents" (verses 9–10).

So lost animals and lost money are used to make the point that, once found, there is happiness, just as God rejoices when lost human beings are "found" in repentance.

The third example sharpens the focus further and directly concerns a lost son, a father, repentance and joy. It's known as the parable of the prodigal son.

Jesus said, "A certain man had two sons. And the younger of them said to his father, 'Father, give me the portion of goods that falls to me.'" His father complied, and the young man went off and squandered the entire inheritance. He wound up finding a job feeding pigs yet was unable to earn enough to feed himself. "But when he came to himself, he said, 'How many of my father's hired servants have bread enough and to spare, and I perish with hunger! I will arise and go to my father, and will say to him, "Father, I have sinned against heaven and before you, and I am no longer worthy to be called your son. Make me like one of your hired servants.'"'" When he returned home, his compassionate father ran to meet him, welcomed him back with open arms, and told the servants, "'Bring out the best robe and put it on him, and put a ring on his hand and sandals on his feet. And bring the fatted calf here and kill it, and let us eat and be merry; for this my son was dead and is alive again; he was lost and is found.' And they began to be merry" (verses 11–24).

This time the reader is left to make the connection between the father in the story and the Father in heaven, who is ready to forgive and rejoice when human beings repent. Notice that the son "came to himself" and said to his father, "I have sinned against heaven and in your sight." Notice that the father ran to meet him once he had begun the process of repentance.

This parable also has a warning in its conclusion about how easy it is to sin against our fellow human beings by being unforgiving when they have already repented before God: When the older son came in from working in the field, he was told by a servant that his brother had returned and that their father had thrown a party in celebration. But the older son resented the fact that his wayward brother should be given special treatment when he himself had always worked hard and obeyed his father, yet he had never been similarly honored. The father explained, "Son, you are always with me, and all that I have is yours. It was right that we should make merry and be glad, for your brother was dead and is alive again, and was lost and is found" (verses 25–32). The older brother was entirely self-focused. Here Jesus is teaching the religious leaders around him that they are guilty of self-righteousness and a lack of compassion. Luke's account sets the scene by saying, "Then all the tax collectors and the sinners drew near to Him to hear Him. And the Pharisees and scribes complained, saying, 'This Man receives sinners and eats with them'" (verses 1–2).

Jesus' three parables are also designed to teach the religious leaders that God is concerned for everyone's happiness in finding forgiveness by turning to the right way. As Peter writes elsewhere, "The Lord is not slack concerning His promise, as some count slackness, but is longsuffering toward us, not willing that any should perish but that all should come to repentance" (2 Peter 3:9).

"If Your Brother Sins Against You"

Shortly after the three parables, Luke records Jesus' teaching about sins that humans commit against each other. Let's look further at the other aspect of lawlessness—that which does not concern God directly, but our fellowman, our neighbor. Jesus said, "Take heed to yourselves. If your brother sins against you, rebuke him; and if he repents, forgive him. And if he sins against you seven times in a day, and seven times in a day returns to you, saying, 'I repent,' you shall forgive him" (Luke 17:3–4).

This is about the responsibilities of the sinner and the one sinned against. Notice that repentance, a change of heart and direction, is still part of the equation for the sinner, as is forgiveness or reconciliation on the part of the one against whom the offense has taken place. The word *forgive* here in the original Greek is *aphiemi*. The related noun *aphesis* means "forgiveness, release, remission" or "letting go of financial debt." Forgiveness in this context can be likened to the release and letting go that comes with the ending of debt.

Matthew's Gospel provides more teaching on the subject for Jesus' followers: "Moreover if your brother sins against you, go and tell him his fault between you and him alone. If he hears you, you have gained your brother. But if he will not hear, take with you one or two more, that 'by the mouth of two or three witnesses every word may be established.' And if he refuses to hear them, tell it to the church. But if he refuses even to hear the church, let him be to you like a heathen and a tax collector" (Matthew 18:15–17).

There is a cutting off of communication at this point, when there is no hearing and thus no repentance.

What has been said by Jesus causes Peter to want to ask a common question: "Lord, how often shall my brother sin against me, and I forgive him? Up to seven times?" Jesus said to him, "I do not say to you, up to seven times, but up to seventy times seven" (verses 21–22).

Of course, Jesus did not mean 490 times! He meant that we should always forgive in the presence of a repentant attitude. Sometimes people will say "I forgive, but I'll never forget." In other words, they do not forgive, but rather harbor bad feelings. The truth about God is that when He forgives, the record is clean. "'Come now, and let us reason together,' says the LORD, 'though your sins are like scarlet, they shall be as white as snow; though they are red like crimson, they shall be as wool'" (Isaiah 1:18). Moreover, "as far as the east is from the west, so far has He removed our transgressions from us" (Psalm 103:12). So everyone must forgive and forget when there is a repentant spirit. Of course, lessons should be learned from the experience, yet divorced from the sinner.

But what if there is no indication of repentance? Then there is certainly no allowance for bearing grudges. Not surprisingly, the law given to ancient Israel about this sounds very much like New Testament teaching: "You shall not hate your brother in your heart. You shall surely rebuke your neighbor, and not bear sin because of him. You shall not take vengeance, nor bear any grudge against the children of your people, but you shall love your neighbor as yourself: I am the LORD" (Leviticus 19:17–18). To "bear any grudge" is translated from the Hebrew *natar*, "to keep or maintain anger." Not holding grudges allows a state of mind that is ready and willing to forgive. Reconciliation is the goal. And if there cannot be reconciliation, an attitude of *willingness* to forgive must be maintained. There can be no excuse for withholding a forgiving spirit and attitude toward others.

The theme of "anger that needs to find an end" is mentioned in Jesus' Sermon on the Mount: "But I say to you that whoever is angry with his brother without a cause shall be in danger of the judgment. And whoever says to his brother, 'Raca!' shall be in danger of the council. But whoever says, 'You fool!' shall be in danger of hell fire. Therefore if you bring your gift to the altar, and there remember that your brother has something against you, leave your gift there before the altar, and go your way. First be reconciled to your brother, and then come and offer your gift" (Matthew 5:22–24).

Forgiven and Forgiving

As stated at the beginning, human forgiveness and God's forgiveness have differences. The main one is that we cannot apply Jesus' sacrifice to someone else's sins. According to the Lord's Prayer, actually a model for prayer, we are to ask for God's forgiveness regularly, just as we are regularly to forgive others who have sinned against us. But human nature is at odds with the convictions of the God-focused mind. As Paul said, "I find then a law, that evil is present with me, the one who wills to do good" (Romans 7:21). He also knew that on his own strength, he could not always do the right thing. But He had to choose to do right and with God's help achieve it.

As long as we will not act upon these truths with respect to forgiveness, from a biblical perspective we cannot have a right relationship with God.

Interview:
Hope Springs Eternal

Ishmael Beah was 12 years old when Sierra Leone's brutal, decade-long civil war reached his village in January 1993. Soon he found himself swept into the army, a child soldier.

Fourteen years later, after rehabilitation, college and a new life with a family in America, Beah spoke with *Vision*'s Gina Stepp and shared some of the insight he'd gained from his experience and his hope that other children can be spared from repeating it. He also talked of forgiveness.

GS After a Southern California earthquake, scientists study to learn why certain buildings may have collapsed. But sometimes we can learn even more from the buildings that didn't collapse. If we see your experience as an "earthquake" and you as one of the strong buildings that survived, what can we learn from you about the factors that enabled you to cope and survive?

IB Well, I believe it had a lot to do with my early upbringing. Growing up in a community that had a very deep appreciation for life and respect for adults, I gained a very strong sense of family tradition. I think because of my early upbringing I developed a sense of self. I was very strong and even through the war, when everything seemed to have been wiped out, there was still something present, because that very short childhood I had was so remarkable.

I was able to go back to it as sort of a foundation to stand upon and outlive what had happened to me.

When I was running from the war, the thing that kept me going at first was the fact that there was family alive somewhere. I had to find them. But when that was no longer the case, I'm not sure what really kept me going. Using your metaphor of the earthquake: particularly during the war I believe that there was nothing I could have done, especially when I was in it, to stay alive. So I believe it was pure luck and the grace of God. At any time it could have been me who was killed, not the person standing next to me. My survival was not because I knew how to run fast, or because I was smart.

After being removed from the war, I think my life changed because of the people who came into my life and who were able to show me that compassion and kindness still existed, and that human beings could deeply care for each other, selflessly. That made me trust in myself again. And I knew there was more to my life than what I'd been taught. A series of things came about, but I guess what I am trying to say is that I didn't do it by myself. There was the support I had early on and there was support that came afterward, and that was very, very important.

There is no "Ishmael formula" in terms of healing. There is no such thing. I think that everyone with the right care and support can [heal], if there are people who are willing to accept them fully into their lives and give them the strength they need to continue living.

GS You had a friend named Saidu. In your book you said he eventually gave up. What was the difference between your outlook and his?

IB   I think in the context of the war, especially as we were running from it, we had to have hope, regardless of how little it was. Even if it meant celebrating just having a chance to stop and drink clean water. Once you lose hope you lose the determination to continue running, during the context of war. Now, this is not just specific to Africa but to any war. You are happy just to receive a loaf of bread, because holding on to that hope gives you strength to live through the next thing. Particularly for Saidu, one of the things that happened was that he lost hope while traveling. He felt that each time someone came upon us and tried to kill us, he lost a part of himself. He couldn't see the possibility that this would end someday, so he lost the strength to continue running. I believe that when your spirit stops striving to move forward you lose hope. When we were running, obviously the situation *was* hopeless, but we always felt that something new could happen. We always hoped, "Oh, tomorrow maybe something will be good." Maybe sometimes we didn't believe it, but we had to *try* to believe it; there was no other choice.

GS   That belief that something could change is what kept you going, then?

IB   That belief that something could change. Because you see, I remembered that when I was a kid, my father used to tell me that "as long as you are alive, there is a possibility for something to change in your life." Now, it could be good or bad, but something *will* change. So when I was running I kept that thought: "If I am still alive there is still hope that this could end and that I could survive." That didn't turn out to be the case for quite a while, but eventually it did.

GS   When you found out that your family was gone, you were still on the run. You've also said you were given no time to think after being pressed into the army. If you didn't have time to think, did you have time to grieve the loss of your family?

IB   Very little. The thing about living in this context was that there was very little time to grieve for the people you lost—and for everything else you lost. But even if there was, that might also kill you because there is so much that you see, and there is so much you're exposed to. Grieving would almost be accepting defeat in a way that, in a normal circumstance, is not the case. No, I wasn't able to grieve until afterward when I was at the rehabilitation center; there I did. But before that I went through the emotion of feeling severe pain, of not wanting to be alive and feelings of that sort, but I didn't have much time to grieve because we had to keep going. Feeling remorseful or being incredibly sad was not something that would propel you forward. The kinds of battles I've seen expose you to so much violence that you learn to block your emotions, to not let them arise. If they take hold of you, you might not be able to do other things.

GS   In line with that, you said in your book that when the memories started coming back during rehabilitation, you had to break through some of those bad memories to get to the good ones?

IB   Yes, it was very difficult, because I'd seen so much that was completely different from what my life had been before, and it was so shocking that it became this permanent block in my head. I could not even think of a life before the war. And so I had to go through those [war] experiences to try and understand, and to make that breakthrough between. Perhaps that is what trauma is. I am not a psychologist so I don't know how to comment on this, but for me I felt like it was a stumbling block that stopped me from connecting to a life that was peaceful and from believing that there was a possibility for that again. After everything I had been exposed to, I had come to believe otherwise.

GS In your book you explained that you were taught by the army to envision the enemy as those who were responsible for killing your family. Even though you did this in battle, none of the killing made you feel better about your loss. Instead you said there was a further loss—a temporary loss of your humanity. Do you feel anger about any of this?

IB Yes, at some point I felt deep anger, but I don't think I'm bitter. I feel anger because I want something to be done to prevent this from happening to other people, and I try to do that. But I'm not angry in the sense that I want the same things that happened to me to happen to them, or that I want them to die or anything. I just don't want this to continue happening to children.

One thing that I learned the hard way, which I hope other people will not learn the hard way: nothing good comes out of this anger, this need for retaliation, for brutal payback. You cannot be in a position to understand how to prevent the problem if you do not speak with those who have hurt you. It's important to try to understand why this fellow who perhaps years before the war would have helped you, would have fed you, would be one of the active members in your community—how did he come to be responsible for doing so much harm to you? I think if you don't engage in a conversation with him, you can't understand that. But I want people to be held accountable, so every now and then I feel angry; it's a common human tendency. But not to the point that I want revenge or anything; that doesn't do anyone any good.

GS   What about forgiveness? Is that concept part of it?

IB   I think a lot of people think forgiving and forgetting comes together. People think forgiving is forgetting everything. From my personal perspective, it's not. Forgiving is, in my opinion, being willing to put a stop to the continuation of the violence itself—to say that, however difficult it is, I am going to stop seeing my neighbor as a perpetual thief or a perpetual killer. Once you do that, you actually *will* live in peace—with yourself as well as with your neighbor. If you see your neighbor as a perpetual thief or a perpetual killer, you can never live in peace alongside him. And that will actually propel you to do something back to him, which will just exacerbate the problem.

So I think forgiving is actually a way of understanding each other better, and trying to solve the problem rather than going about in a very fearful manner among people. Now, it's not easy; it's very difficult. It's easy to say, "Oh, forgive this, forgive that." But forgiveness comes with other things as well. For example, in Sierra Leone you cannot ask people to forgive if they have to go and resettle in the ruins of the village that reminds them of that hurt over and over. It's difficult. Forgiving also comes from rebuilding and empowering people so they can continue with their lives. So there is that aspect of it.

But it's not about forgetting. I think being aware allows us to be in a position to prevent it from happening again; to be in a position to pinpoint when things are about to erupt. Not necessarily to be obsessed with it, but to have it in the back of your mind as a constant reminder of how fragile life is, which becomes very apparent when you find yourself in a conflict situation. Life is very fragile; you are not in control as much is you think you are. Only by working as a community can you even be in a little better control—in your life and the lives of others around you as well.

GS When you went to the rehabilitation center, it made you a little angry at first when they kept saying nothing was your fault. At the time you couldn't understand why they were saying this. But in the end it was their compassion— you said it was the fact that they were willing to see you as children—that won you over. Why do you think that particular thing made such a difference?

IB Well, because coming from the experience, I believed that people didn't care about each other for their own benefit, and that adults particularly would use children. But it was also due to being in a series of deceptions; for example, you've lost your family, and then this group that you've come to believe was your surrogate family—you are plucked away from them. So there is a lot of hurt, and you do not want to trust or believe in anyone. But the willingness of the staff at this place to look at us just as kids, regardless of what we had done—they were willing to see *us*. In the beginning it was actually very upsetting, but as time went on we began to see that these were people who genuinely cared about us. When you're a child who has been through difficulties, that is one of the things you learn: to determine when somebody really cares for you. You can size people up pretty easily when you walk into a room; you have that ability. Survival tactics are built into you. And you test people to see whether their concern is concrete, because you are so used to people coming and going in your life—of people not being there—that you want to make sure somebody really does care. So when a staff member would go and come back, and go and come back, even though we would hurt them and try to push them away, as time went on we realized that they really did care about us, and that changed something within us.

GS   You tested them with violence?

IB   Well, the only methods that we knew for testing them were violent; we had been conditioned to behave that way for many years, so that became our only outlet.

GS   You said at one point, when the memories started to come back, that some of the things you had been involved with made you cringe. Did the fact that some things were actually able to touch your conscience in that way help the healing process?

IB   Yes, I think it did. When I started writing the book, the aim was not necessarily for it to be a healing process for me. But as the process went on I realized that actually it was, for lack of a better word, therapeutic for me, in the sense that I had to revisit certain things when I was no longer traumatized, or under the influence of drugs or coercion, to really kind of feel and understand what it is that I was forced to be a part of. And I think that made me understand a lot about the nature of violence itself, and, as human beings, how susceptible we all are to it. So I think in that sense, yes, I did heal quite a bit.

GS   And as you help other people by talking to them, telling them about the things you went through—is this helping you heal too?

IB   Yes. Well, for me, I think healing has been complete in the sense that I have learned to live with the past. I could never forget; but I have learned to live with the memories and I've learned to transform them, so that the goal of my talking about it is to expose it. As I speak to you, more and more kids are going through these things. I don't want that to happen. So for me, the extraordinary luck of surviving and of having a family that took me in, and having an education—I want to use that to help others. For me that's what it is about. And along the way, if I get some psychological healing, I think that's okay.

GS The trauma experts say that taking an active role is a big part of healing, so it seems you're doing that.

IB I certainly hope so.

GS You've been talking about not wanting this to keep happening. What's really going to change the problem?

IB Well, what we are really working for is enough political will in the international scene to prevent these wars from actually occurring. Preventive measures—because once war has started in most places, eventually women and children will get abused, and children will get recruited. That's the natural progression. So it's the preventive aspect that we are working toward. That's a long-term goal, because most nations are not interested in doing anything that doesn't directly affect them and their people. But a short-term goal is to actually help the children who have been affected or the people in the communities that have been affected. In a lot of places that's possible; people are doing it effectively. And by doing so, perhaps we can lessen the number of children who go into soldiering. Also, there is a way of enhancing international standards that bring people to justice, and this is being done.

Now, I'm not naïve; the problem is big. It's a global issue, so sometimes even when five, six, seven solid steps are taken, it seems as if nothing is happening, because this problem is so big. But I don't want anyone to despair, because I think it's possible to prevent the use of children in war, as long as we create enough public awareness and bring enough government attention to it.

GS Some of your friends actually passed through rehabilitation and went back to the army. This was because they didn't have families to go back to, right? What can be done to stop the problem at that point?

IB Well, there are two reasons. First of all, they went back because there was still a war going on during the rehabilitation process. Because they weren't put up with good foster families that were able to take care of them, they didn't have a place to go. Now, this part of the rehabilitation process is one of the things that I've been trying to advocate as well. They have a short-term goal, which is that they rehabilitate the children and then drop them into society. There needs to be a follow-up. So that is also very important; just putting the kids through the process of psychological therapy is not enough. You have to give them something to live for. They need to go to school to learn something. When they don't have those things—they already have the military expertise, and the conflict is all around them—the tendency to go back is greater.

Ishmael Beah graduated from Oberlin College in 2004. He has spoken before many national and international organizations, including the United Nations and the Council on Foreign Relations, and serves on the advisory committee of the Human Rights Watch Children's Rights Division.

RELATED ARTICLES AT WWW.VISION.ORG:

"Child Soldiers"

"Repercussions of Revenge" (Book review: *A Long Way Gone: Memoirs of a Boy Soldier*)

"A Former Child Soldier's View of Forgiveness" (*Vision* video interview with Ishmael Beah, author of *A Long Way Gone*)

Interview: The Many Faces of Forgiveness

"Given that wrong-doing is pervasive in human affairs," writes philosophy professor Charles L. Griswold, "the question as to whether (and how) to forgive presents itself continuously" (*Forgiveness: A Philosophical Exploration*, Cambridge University Press, 2007).

But because of an endless range of theological and philosophical ideas about what forgiveness means, finding a productive way forward—whether we have wronged someone or have been wronged—isn't always easy. Still, says Griswold, "the daily fact of wrong-doing" requires us to do just that.

In this interview with *Vision* publisher David Hulme, the Boston University professor explores the subject of forgiveness: what it is, what it isn't, and how it plays out in our politicized world as well as in our individual lives.

DH Why did you decide to write a book about forgiveness?

CG Philosophers have in recent years returned to writing about some of the great issues of human life. There's now a whole literature on the nature of happiness, which is a classic philosophical theme. There's also a lot of recent work in philosophy on issues of mortality and even the meaning of life. Forgiveness is a very important moral notion in common life. Like a number of philosophers, I want to bring the skills and resources of my discipline to bear on these great issues.

There's also an intellectual as well as a biographical reason for writing the book. In my early years as a scholar, I worked a lot on Plato and the issue of Platonic perfectionism. I've become very dissatisfied with perfectionist moral and political theories that want us to judge things according to some standard of superhuman perfection. I started to think through alternatives that accept the fundamental imperfections of human life and respond to them constructively. My turn to forgiveness was an effort to understand what virtues would go well with an acceptance of the ineluctable imperfections of the world but avoided resignation or quietism in response to them, or an effort to flee to some other world. It became clear to me that forgiveness is indeed one such virtue.

On the biographical side, like most people who reach middle age, you wake up one day and realize that you've both realized a great deal of wrongdoing and done some yourself. This, to me, raises the question of forgiveness. Also, you've probably been part of—in one way or another—decisions that have caused hurt, or you've been the recipient of such decisions. Those, too, raise the question of forgiveness. I was divorced about eight years ago, and it was just then that I began to think all the more insistently on this question—whether one could forgive wrongs and be forgiven.

DH Has writing about the subject changed you in any way?

CG It's probably not for me to pronounce whether I'm more or less forgiving, but I'm certainly much clearer about what it means to forgive and what it is that I'm doing when I put aside anger at someone for having done me wrong, or anger on behalf of someone who has been wronged. On the political side, the distinction between forgiveness and apology wasn't at all clear to me before. Now that I have a worked-out view about that, my judgment about what's appropriate in the political sphere is also much clearer than it used to be.

DH What do you expect your readers to go away with?

CG A new understanding of why forgiveness is a virtue, under what conditions it's a virtue, what it means to forgive, the conditions that both parties to the transaction must meet, and how forgiveness differs from other concepts that are part of the same family of ideas and are easily confused with it; for example, excuse, pardon, mercy, apology and so forth.

DH When we hear the word *forgiveness,* a lot of us think of it in some sort of theological sense. But your approach is secular. Can you elaborate on the difference between the two perspectives?

CG The term does have religious connotations, and I would say that there are many different religious views of it, not just one. How it fits into Judaism, for example, is an extremely interesting question. I don't think it fits in the same way as it does in Christianity. How does it fit into Islam? What role does it have in Buddhism? Did it have any role in Greek or Roman polytheism? So there's not just one but many religious views, and they may not be compatible with each other. Even within the history of Christianity, I strongly suspect that there are actually competing views of the notion.

In spite of this, I don't see any reason why one couldn't work out a secular view of the subject—which doesn't depend on the assertion that God doesn't exist but just suspends judgment about the religious dimension. The logic of such a view is going to be quite different from the logic of a view that assumes the existence of God or gods.

DH How do you respond to the claim that the Judeo-Christian ethic provides a richer understanding because it brings in forgiveness from a very different direction—from a God-being?

CG I think that assertion is false. Show me that this other view is richer, and explain to me what "richer" means. I don't think it's richer; I think it's different. I suspect that the Judaic and the Christian views themselves differ from each other. The key point that is often made for the thesis that the Christian view is richer or superior—to speak in these broad generalizations—is that if you assume there is a forgiving God, you have a solution to a set of problems that the secular view can't solve. It is held that the Christian view allows a kind of unconditional forgiveness—forgiveness no matter what the wrongdoer does—and that the model for this is God, who forgives unconditionally. If you are unable to forgive some terrible wrong, you receive a kind of moral or spiritual support from God, who helps you to forgive, or God does the forgiving for you if you can't, thereby giving the wrongdoer a new lease on life, or a new chance for a moral life. The claim is that the secular view doesn't allow for that, and that that's a defect.

DH I distinguish between biblical principle and what we are calling Christian principle; I don't think they're necessarily the same thing. Jesus and Paul had the Hebrew Scriptures as their basis. The widely accepted Christian perspective that comes from early church fathers such as Origen or Augustine may be antithetical to biblical definition.

CG Yes. A colleague, Ilaria Ramelli, is writing a paper for a volume of essays that asks "Is forgiveness unconditional when you look at early Christianity?" And her answer is going to be no, and that it's a later development. Not even God forgives unconditionally. There are all kinds of things you're supposed to do, such as repent, etc.

DH In your book you make the point that political apology is not the same as asking for forgiveness.

CG Yes. I think of forgiveness in an interpersonal context. It's about a moral response on the part of a victim to a wrongdoer. Issues of anger and resentment are at stake, of recognition, of respect; evidence to the effect that a person is really changing his or her ways and thereby earning forgiveness—that's at stake; and a whole set of moral ideals are at play also, which have to do with holding people to certain moral standards and living those standards by becoming changed people.

Apology is certainly part of interpersonal forgiveness, but in the political context you can have apology without forgiveness: apology does require taking responsibility, but accepting it doesn't require giving up resentment. It requires giving up revenge, but you could genuinely accept an apology without giving up resentment. I think that's appropriate to the dynamics of a political context, and also the fact that the transaction is often taking place not between two individuals but between an individual and a corporate entity, or two such entities—nations or corporations or churches. In the book I look at the case of President Clinton apologizing on behalf of the United States to the Japanese Americans who were wrongly interned during World War II, and to their descendents. President Clinton had nothing to do personally with the wrong in question. So he's uttering an apology as the representative of an entity, many of whose current members also had nothing to do with it. And some of the people to whom he's offering the apology were not themselves in the camps. That doesn't mean that the apology is not real or morally important; it's just different from what's going on in the interpersonal context of forgiveness.

DH What you're after here is more a case of linguistic precision, isn't it?

CG It is a case of linguistic and conceptual precision, but it's not just semantics, because the conditions for the satisfactory execution of an apology are not the same as for forgiveness, though some of them overlap. In political apology as well as forgiveness, a commitment is made to the idea that the truth should be told. So when you apologize, the idea is to state what it is you're apologizing for, which entails making the facts of the matter publicly accessible. So too in forgiveness: if I forgive you for such-and-such, you will have asked for forgiveness and also stated what it is that you're asking forgiveness for. But the individual who did the wrong doesn't have to be the one who's apologizing for it, or the individual who receives the apology could do so on behalf of someone else. And the way in which it connects with a moral sentiment such as resentment is quite different. So the distinction is not just semantic.

DH Do you see the 2008 Australian government apology to the aboriginal people in the same terms as the Clinton administration's apology to Japanese Americans?

CG Yes. And by the way, from the account I read in the newspapers, the Australian prime minister's apology was well done because it was very explicit in taking corporate responsibility, stating that it really is a wrong and that the government really is apologizing for it. It also put on record the wrong that was done.

DH Whereas in the case of President Richard Nixon, you have a very different perspective.

CG President Nixon never really apologized. David Frost asked him in the famous interview, "Do you apologize?" and Nixon said something like "There could be no greater apology than resigning from the presidency." That's a classic evasion. You could resign the presidency for all kinds of reasons. That's not an apology. To apologize you've got to say that you apologize.

DH One of the things that stands out in seeking forgiveness is that it has to be from the heart, and the forgiving has to be from the heart. How does that play into the kind of secular virtue that you're discussing?

CG It plays directly into it. I don't use that metaphor, but what it's getting at is compatible with what I'm saying. In a successful interpersonal scene of forgiveness, the wrongdoer truly changes his or her ways in addition to providing an explanation for how he or she came to do the wrong, as well as understanding how it affected the other individual. So a real commitment to change is shown in word and deed. But the same is also true on the part of the wronged, because the wronged person not only gives up revenge but changes internally by letting go of what was warranted anger. But they also change their view of the wrongdoer. This is referred to in the philosophical literature as "reframing." You come to see the wrongdoer in a different way. These are fundamental changes. They are "from the heart," if you like.

DH Can an individual seek forgiveness from a group? Let's take the savings-and-loan executive who pillages his clients' accounts, then asks for forgiveness. Let's suppose it is indeed from the heart. Does that fit in with your model?

CG I think it's certainly possible and appropriate to apologize, and to apologize from the heart. But the idea of being forgiven by an abstract entity like a group doesn't make sense to me. I don't think groups forgive. Individuals do the forgiving.

DH You're saying that in some instances the popular model of forgiveness just doesn't fit, and that in certain cases an apology could be viewed as equivalent to seeking forgiveness.

CG That's correct, and I think it's very useful to know that. That's one of the ways in which this philosophical analysis can help us understand what is appropriate to demand and not to demand in various contexts. And this is also true of reparations. None of the above touches the issue of justice. The loan executive who stole the depositors' money—no matter what he or she does with respect to apology or forgiveness—may still have to meet the requirements of justice. For example, he may need to compensate the people whose money he took, or serve time in jail, or whatever is appropriate. No amount of apology or forgiveness obviates the need for considerations of justice where appropriate.

DH This brings in the concept of mercy, and what mercy is and isn't. It has often occurred to me that this is where people get tangled up; they want to be soft-hearted but end up being soft-headed. People have an indistinct view of what it means to forgive, and they never get to the point of justice.

CG I would agree with that. If we're embezzlers and we both get caught and both apologize, but your depositors happen to be given to mercy and successfully ask the court not to prosecute or punish you, whereas mine are not and I get punished for the exact same crime that you committed— that really raises a question of fairness, and it is soft-headed to wave it away on grounds that mercy is a virtue. It's not that there's no room for mercy or clemency in a judicial context, but it shouldn't trump considerations that are appropriate to that context.

DH I raise it because you also talk about a *culture* of apology and forgiveness that seems to have developed. How has that happened, and what are its pros and cons?

CG I suspect it's come about recently as a product of the self-help therapeutic movement on the one hand and a certain interpretation of Christianity on the other. And there's a lot of overlap between the two. If you look at the mountains of nonphilosophical literature on forgiveness, you'll often see an overlap between the self-help approach and a religious or Christian view emphasizing unconditional forgiveness. It also has deep roots in notions of compassion, of public transparency, and of an expectation that people in political life will be responsive to the people. It's probably part of a flowering of democratic culture, and one could probably learn a lot about how this happened by reading people like de Tocqueville, but I haven't done a sociological study of the matter and indeed don't know of one.

As to the pros and the cons, in the book I talk about some of the dangers that this sort of culture is open to, and one of them is that forgiveness and apology become merely theatrical. They cease being heartfelt, which robs them of much of their moral seriousness. There's even the worry that once forgiveness and apology become expected in the culture and in the public sphere, they become coerced, with punishments for not performing correctly.

DH Is it possible to apologize to people who are dead, for wrongs others have committed toward them?

CG That's a complicated question, because it involves not just the matter of apologizing to the dead but apologizing on behalf of *others* to the dead. Third-party forgiveness is built in to such a question. That introduces one set of considerations, but the other is whether—third-party or not—it makes any sense to apologize to the dead. I would say yes, and indeed it's possible under some conditions to be *forgiven* by the dead. I know that sounds strange initially, but imagine the mirror case: you've been wronged by someone who then died, and you find on their deathbed an elaborate letter of apology and contrition and a credible statement that, had the person lived, they would have taken all the appropriate steps to seek your forgiveness. They have now died. Is it possible to forgive such a person? I think so, if you can construct a narrative of the sort just indicated.

So, too, in the case of apologizing to people who are dead. If one could construct a narrative according to which they would receive it—and thereby alleviate one's guilt— and if one genuinely takes other important steps to warrant forgiveness, then why shouldn't it be possible to imagine them as forgiving you for good reason? But these are imperfect cases of apology and forgiveness. What I mean is that one would wish for the person to not be dead and to apologize to someone who could receive it, or to be able to forgive someone who had earned that forgiveness at the right moment and in the right way.

DH When we talk about forgiveness, we're usually talking about giving up resentment toward someone else. What about people who say "Well, I'll forgive but I'll never forget." Their meaning is that they are still bearing a great deal of resentment. They haven't in fact forgiven.

CG Right! That is indeed *not* forgiving. You can't forgive and continue to boil away with active resentment. Giving up that resentment is part of forgiveness. So if by not forgetting you mean still remaining resentful, then that's a contradiction.

DH Bearing grudges enters the picture here. One of the big challenges in life is that you often have situations where people show no remorse; they've wronged you but they'll never face it. How do you go about the rest of your life with that sort of memory? It's difficult if you don't come to terms with the fact that it is possible to live life without bearing grudges. Is it possible to be in a condition of "preparedness to forgive"?

CG It is a perplexing and maddening situation when you've been wronged and the other person will not take even the most elementary steps to earn your forgiveness. Some version of that is probably the norm, unfortunately. So we often are stuck in a situation where we would like to forgive, in principle, but in a sense are prevented from doing so. Forgiveness is not the magic bullet for solving all of these issues—including responding to the unapologetic wrongdoing and the toxicity of the anger that one feels in response. There are other things one then has to do: these range from therapy, to forgetting, to somehow moving past, possibly to excusing and constructing some kind of narrative that explains why this person is incapable of apologizing—say, that the person is morally and psychologically damaged, and trying to find some way to excuse them on that basis (which is different from forgiving them). I think there's a whole range of responses that one might need to adopt for this very common problem.

DH So if a person won't admit wrong, it's very difficult for us to actually forgive; in fact, it's illogical.

CG What you're actually doing is *not* forgiving. And again, this isn't just a semantic point—it does make a difference what you call it.

I think there's another profound issue here about whether people do wrong knowingly or not. Everything I've said about forgiveness depends on the thesis that in some sense of the term, people do wrong knowingly (at least some of the time). If you're a Socratic, you would argue that the thesis is false and that people, when they do wrong, actually don't know that it is wrong. They think it's good, or right. And if that's true, then the appropriate response isn't forgiveness but understanding and excusing.

DH It could also be not bearing a grudge as a consequence.

CG Absolutely. And I think excusing can effect a lessening of resentment or anger. Whether it *requires* forswearing anger is something that I haven't worked out. It probably does, but I'd have to think about that.

DH Is forgiveness essential to reconciliation?

CG: It all depends on what you mean by reconciliation. If you mean cessation of hostilities, then no. People cease hostilities for all kinds of reasons that don't involve forgiveness. You might just cease it momentarily to gain the advantage or to avoid disadvantage; or you're fed up with war, and some kind of modus vivendi is preferable. None of that involves forgiveness.

If by reconciliation you mean something more like the resumption of the previous relationship in an interpersonal context, then the tie-in is much closer. I would certainly say that the goal of forgiveness is reconciliation and that accomplished forgiveness does reconcile, but I wouldn't say that every kind of reconciliation is dependent on forgiveness.

DH It comes back to the precursor being some form of repentance and what we were talking about earlier—something coming from the heart. If you get yourself to the point that you're willing to take on a forgiving approach with the nuances you've suggested, it seems that would lead to other changes in behavior—the ancient Hebrew concept of *shub*: turning around and going the other way. So we're back to the connection between religious concepts and secular virtues, because we are dealing with the values part of our life.

CG Yes, I agree entirely with that. It would be very interesting to do a cross-cultural analysis of forgiveness in different religious contexts. For example, I don't think there's much room for forgiveness in ancient Greek thought, which was heavily religious (except among the philosophers, and even then moral reflection was often religious in some sense). There exists a very rich mine of research on this issue of religions and forgiveness, yet to be explored systematically and philosophically.

RELATED ARTICLE AT WWW.VISION.ORG:

"Forgiveness (or Something Like It)"

A Change of Mind

Researchers have thought for years that the brain comes prewired, but new findings suggest otherwise.

"A man convinced against his will is of the same opinion still"; "Where there's a will, there's a way"—two familiar ways of expressing what is commonly known about the ease or difficulty we have in changing our minds in lasting ways.

The role of the will in change of heart and mind is part and parcel of the conceptual framework we use to explain how our decision making is affected by our own independent thought processes. Unless we believe that everything in human life is predetermined, then we must acknowledge that human beings have free moral agency. We are not irreversibly programmed by our genes nor by our early environment; we can make changes in our existence by conscious, willed thought leading to action. How exactly this process is reflected in the physical structure of the brain has become known only recently.

Researchers thought for years that the brain came prewired—that its development from birth through adolescence was the result of a gradual unfolding of its already existing potential and that by adulthood it was set. But new findings have shown that the brain's circuitry is wired as the individual develops and can be *rewired* by the conscious thought of the individual. In other words, we can change our own patterns of thought and behavior by our own self-directed will. The evidence of this is observable in physical changes in the neural pathways of the brain. These new circuits can become fixed and replace previous pathways.

The capacity of the brain to rewire itself is termed its "neuroplasticity." The first inklings of this phenomenon came with work on stroke victims and with people suffering from obsessive-compulsive disorder (OCD). It became clear that certain patients, parts of whose brain circuitry had been compromised by cerebral hemorrhage leaving them unable to perform specific tasks, could be retrained. Their brain circuits would rewire a way around the particular problem. This took intensive training, but it produced positive and permanent changes. Those suffering from OCD (for example, uncontrollable hand-washing resulting from a fear of germs) found relief once they understood that part of their brain circuitry was causing the problem. They were trained in the technique of using their own self-directed free will to rewire their faulty circuitry.

It goes without saying that such breakthroughs are needed in other mental and behavioral impasses. The new findings have profound implications for improvement in the most difficult and sensitive human problems from depression to addictions of all kinds and even protracted national and international deadlocks. The severely depressed can be helped by undertaking the Four Steps program, in which they learn to recognize what is happening inside their brains and take appropriate self-directed or willed actions. In other findings, there is the possibility of using the self-directed will to shut down the sexual response in those obsessed with pornography.

There is a spiritual parallel to these new findings. That there are nonphysical principles behind physical change in the brain is clear when we take into consideration the ancient Hebrew verb *shub*, which means "to (re)turn." One of its primary additional meanings is to repent of wrong actions before God by turning away from evil. The word combines two aspects of repentance: to turn from evil and to turn to the good. This means that we retrace our steps and find the right way again. We may define evil very broadly as anything that damages our relationship with God or man (including oneself). In other words, those activities of our minds and bodies that harm us, others around us, and our relationship with God are evil and need to be changed first at the level of the mind, by the use of the will to do good. In the case of the ancient Israelites, God wanted them to change their ways by first changing their minds. The *Theological Wordbook of the Old Testament* explains that "by turning, a God-given power, a sinner can redirect his destiny." Another way of saying it is that sin can be overcome through change at the conscious level of the mind when the will is engaged. When the brain's circuits are wired incorrectly, either through damage or conscious choice, harm is done. Change, or rewiring, is the only way forward, the way to health both physically and spiritually.

The New Testament equivalent of *shub* is the Greek verb *metanoeo*. It includes the concept of changing one's mind, or of coming to a new way of thinking. What we have not understood until recently is the role of the physical brain in this process. Once the will to change is engaged and specific actions are taken, new neural pathways are created and new attitudes and new behaviors result. The more we take the new action, the more lasting the behavior becomes. We've had clues about rewiring the brain and our behavior before. It's a common notion that it takes three weeks to break a habit and instill a new one. We know, too, that when we act in harmful or wrong ways regularly, our consciences become seared, and evil gains our acceptance. The way out of human problems as diverse as obsessive-compulsive disorder, bad habits, racial prejudice, hate crimes, depression, brutality, and exploitation of others remains a fundamental change of mind. The Judeo-Christian Scriptures have told us that in principle all along.

As we have seen, that tradition speaks of repentance as introspecting and changing our way of doing so that change is lasting. According to brain researcher Jeffrey Schwartz, his therapeutic technique for treating OCD is very much akin to the biblical concept of repentance: "It's a restatement of what I'm talking about! That is repentance properly understood!" But he also recognizes that the notion of repentance is not in fashion and needs to be. "You cannot form trustful relations with others without acknowledging error, without sincerity," he says. "And when you get right down to it, repentance is a form of sincerity. It's saying, 'I realize I made errors. I'm not perfect. There are things I could try to do better.'"

RELATED ARTICLE AT WWW.VISION.ORG:

"Beyond the Deadlock"

Interview: Fusing Mind and Matter

For some time, conventional science has considered the human mind to be nothing more than an illusion. But Jeffrey M. Schwartz is among a handful of researchers who believe that there's more to the mind than meets the eye.

In 2004 David Hulme interviewed Schwartz, who is a research psychiatrist at the UCLA School of Medicine in Los Angeles and the author of a number of books on brain research.

DH What are we to understand by the term *neuroplasticity*?
JS It means that environmental factors change how the brain works. If you take simple animals such as rodents and put them in an enriched environment, you can see that physical changes occur in the brain. This becomes really interesting in "self-directed neuroplasticity." Humans have the unique capacity to take advantage of these rewiring mechanisms. People can learn to change how their brain responds to circumstances by focusing their attention differently. Focus of attention influences how the brain responds to phenomena, and those changes leave physical traces that you can see with brain imaging.
DH Has the concept of self-directed neuroplasticity been known for long?

JS   No. In fact, I coined the term in my [2002] book, *The Mind and the Brain*, which was co-authored with Sharon Begley of the *Wall Street Journal*. The explanation for *how* the mind can change the brain was first elaborated in collaboration with my physics colleague, Henry Stapp. It turns out that quantum physics has a very coherent way of explaining how attention can change how the brain works— how attention can hold functioning brain circuits in place.

What I did was to make a theoretical model to describe what was happening. It shows that in a condition where there are actually symptoms caused by known brain problems such as obsessive-compulsive disorder [OCD] or stroke, you can train people to respond in ways that have therapeutic results. You actually change the underlying wiring of the brain so that the problem is ameliorated.

Now, in a psychiatric condition where the primary problem has to do with thinking and emotional feelings, that really becomes important. In OCD, people get intrusive, unwanted thoughts. In the '80s we took brain pictures that showed that the bottom of the front of the brain, called the orbital frontal cortex, was overactive, and that there was a gearshift mechanism that was broken in a structure called the caudate nucleus. We used this brain information to get people to understand better that the intrusive, unwanted thoughts were caused by a medical condition: it was a brain wiring problem that was causing them to get these ideas. That helped them to recognize even more clearly that these ideas had nothing to do with *them*. When they started to respond differently with that knowledge (which took training and effort), not only did their clinical condition improve, but they also changed the underlying brain wiring pattern in the orbital frontal cortex and the caudate nucleus. So the way you think about your situation, and the way you respond, and the effort you make to focus your attention differently based on knowledge, literally rewires how your brain works.

DH How does this compare with the use of negative reinforcement to treat compulsive disorders?

JS   Well, that never really worked. But there were other behaviorist approaches that were very effective, using a method called "exposure and response prevention." My difficulty with that was that it didn't take advantage of people's capacity to recognize that the symptoms are false messages from their brain—that the symptoms are really just caused by a medical condition. The mechanical behavioral interventions that behaviorism used, while effective, required the person to go through a lot of anxiety, so they were extremely difficult for people to do on their own. I explained to people with OCD that they could respond differently to those intrusive thoughts and urges. That would not only change their brain, it also would empower them to not be a slave to their brain.

The word I use for the introspection part of the therapy is *mindfulness*—looking inside yourself with the rational, calm perspective of an outside, impartial, fair-minded observer. That allows you to get outside of the fear.

DH Mindfulness is a Buddhist concept. Are you a Buddhist?

JS   No, I'm Jewish, but I am very serious about practicing Buddhist meditation. I've been doing it for going on 30 years.

DH How does your Jewish side connect with Buddhism? How do these two worlds come together for you?

JS   On an ethnic level, I certainly view myself as Jewish, and that's why I like to refer to the Buddhist side as more of a philosophy rather than a religious belief that might conflict with my Jewish identity. I view Buddhism as a scientific, philosophical practice and Judaism more as my core identity. The Buddhist philosophy is framed in a way that is very analytical and technically elaborated. I found explanations involving words like *karma* (which means "will"), *mindfulness, wise, unwise* and *attention,* and the fact that these kinds of wise and unwise attentions will very much influence the moral qualities that people act with. That isn't unique to Buddhist philosophy. It is entirely consistent with things you'll read in the Torah and the Talmud. The new thing was that Buddhism allowed an alignment with modern scientific psychology, and especially with brain mechanisms, because of the stress on introspective, mindful awareness and how much that kind of mental action could be applied in a systematic way.

What I found was that my very strongly believed Judeo-Christian moral belief system was not only consistently confirmed in the Buddhist moral system, but also that I now had a bridge to science. This has always been the culturally difficult part. Science has always been presented as amoral or empirical to the point of not making value judgments. The other thing that's very interesting about Buddhist philosophy is that it has a strong mind-matter interaction component. It says that mind moves and affects matter, while also allowing, in a way that's consistent with modern science, that matter can influence mind as well.

DH This takes you a long way from the traditional Cartesian approach within scientific thought.

JS There's one huge problem with the Cartesian perspective: It views mind and matter as two separate things, and that turns out to be a very bad mistake. Descartes set up two substances, mind and matter, and he tried to finesse a way to get them connected, but he never really did it very successfully. Matter is extended. You can hold it in your hand. Mind is immaterial; it's experiential. Viewing them as separate substances, with science investigating the material, and religion and the spiritual being relevant to the mental side, really created an artificial split in Western civilization that has had negative implications. At the very least, it's outlived its usefulness.

The advantage of this newer way of thinking, with self-directed neuroplasticity based in mindfulness—this quantum physics model of mind-brain relation—is that it does not take the perspective that mind and matter are two intrinsically different things. It views them as an integrable unified reality. The big advantage of quantum physics is that it answers the problem that Descartes (and the entire philosophical tradition for nearly half a millennium after Descartes) had never been able to address: integrating the terms we use when we describe our experiences—pain, pleasure, happiness, sadness, the sense of knowing, the sense of understanding, the sense that life has meaning. These are very real things. In fact, they're the things that make life worthwhile. None of those kinds of terms are translatable into material terms. What the quantum physics allowed us to do was to show how, by taking a mental perspective and having it influence your focus of attention, you could literally hold the brain circuitry (the physical manifestation of the mental experience) in place. In the end, the common denominator of all our experiential reality is how we focus our attention. We choose what parts of our experience we focus on. We choose what parts grab us and take control of us, like greed or ill will; or on the other hand, we let them go by and focus on wholesome, community-oriented acts.

And that's where neuroplasticity kicks in. We know that any repeated action causes the brain to rewire. It's the same as Hebb's rule: basically, brain cells that fire together, wire together. That's all very well established science. Now, what we've done is simply show how focus of attention can get the brain circuits to fire together and then wire together; that's the basic building mechanism whereby you restructure your brain. So this whole mind-brain dichotomy disappears, and what we have is an integrated view of mind-brain as one organically interacting spiritual-material unity.

DH So, no "ghost in the machine."

JS That term was coined by [British philosopher] Gilbert Ryle in what he felt was a great fit of cleverness. It attempted to make it look like anyone who wasn't understanding reality just from five-sense data was locked in phantasmagorias— some primitive, archaic way of thinking where you believe in ghosts. It's the kind of thing that modern, scientifically oriented people aren't supposed to believe in. Well, this is utter nonsense, because the thing that went out the window with "the ghost" was any concept of willfully directed attention.

The explanation I'm putting forward has nothing whatsoever to do with a ghost in the machine. It has to do with the fact that we all have conscious awareness and the capacity to focus that awareness. It's the opposite of ghostlike; it's as clear as the clearest sunshiny day. You can pick out things in your field of vision and focus on them; and you can certainly pick out behavioral choices and focus on those.

DH You say that your approach helps various maladies like stroke, Tourette's Syndrome, tinnitus and dyslexia. Can we add depression and other maladies to the list?

JS Oh, absolutely! Especially now with mindfulness-based cognitive therapy. We should also add things like panic disorder and phobias. Another colleague, Mario Beauregard, has done some extremely interesting research in normal people, showing that we have the full capacity to turn off and on the sexual arousal systems in response to erotic stimuli just by emotionally distancing ourselves. In other words, we make choices about that too. I think we can use that to teach younger people about sexual abstinence training.

DH You used the word *spiritual* a few minutes ago. That's unusual for a scientist.

JS It is, but I don't think it needs to be. That's a cultural phenomenon that needs to change. It's important to stress that it wasn't always so by any stretch of the imagination. If you go back about 125 years, before science really got caught up in this cult of materialism, scientists were perfectly comfortable to talk about the spiritual parts of their nature, even though they might say, once they walked into the laboratory, that they weren't exactly sure about how to address those questions in a scientific context. But we've made advances, because when I talk about spirit, I'm not talking about ectoplasm. I'm simply talking about practical, willful action. When I talk about spiritual practice, I'm talking about the fact that belief guides what we do. In that way, faith can be rational, faith can be experiential, faith can be verified to a greater or lesser extent. It's certainly not a matter of blind faith.

When we strive to do good, that's precisely what I mean by spiritual action. When I talk about spiritual truths, I simply mean that the human mind has the capacity to intuitively recognize that charitable, helpful, nongreedy, nonharming actions are wholesome actions. Actions that are based in greed and ill will and rigid ignorance are unwholesome actions. People know these things, and they also know that these kinds of truths have spiritual content, because they influence the way we direct our willful actions. So in that way it all becomes part of a broader scientific worldview.

DH In your book *Dear Patrick*, you speak to "recovering our souls." What do you mean by this?

JS Just the sense that we are getting back to what we know is true about the distinction between right and wrong, between wholesome and unwholesome actions. We live in a culture that is relativistic and advocates that there is no such thing as moral truth. People have become disconnected from their inner sense that there is a moral reality. The elite secular culture of Western civilization, through the excessive pursuit of self-gratification, has lost contact with the basic truth that to live a happy life you have to have a core connectedness with moral truth. Does it take effort? You bet it takes effort. But we have this capacity for mindful awareness, for honest introspection, for asking ourselves, "Is what I'm doing here wholesome or unwholesome?" Without spending the effort to ask yourself that question, you can degenerate into living an animal life. One of my biggest problems with the way the materialist culture has gone is that it encourages people to view themselves as no different in principle than animals. It encourages people to follow physical pleasure as if that is some ultimate determinant of the difference between what makes life worthwhile and what makes it a burden. These messages have taken their toll, and young people are looking at their elders and saying, "You've given us a false set of values." These false values are based on materialism. There's been a lot of rebellion against that and a real return to spirituality among young people in the United States.

DH Steven Pinker writes that the new discoveries in neuroscience explain what makes us what we are and also invite us to ponder who we want to be.

JS I only wish he would take that seriously, because he has a whole chapter in his book saying that determinism must be true. If determinism is true, what he's describing is not going to have any efficacy. He's trying to have it both ways. We, on the other hand, will take that quote at face value and say that we now know from quantum physics that you actually can do what he's saying there and have it make a difference in how your brain works.

DH The Judeo-Christian tradition talks about repentance, the ancient Hebrew concept of introspecting and changing one's way of doing something so that it's a lasting change— which is really what repentance in its totality means. How does that play into what you're talking about?

JS It's a restatement of what I'm talking about! That is repentance properly understood! In this modern, secular society, there is a media elite culture that tends to view the word *repentance* as if it's some leftover, guilt-laden practice from a benighted past. In the cynical modern age, they say "Never explain; never apologize." That is a prescription for profound dissatisfaction. You cannot form trustful relations with others without acknowledging error, without sincerity. And repentance is just, when you get right down to it, a form of sincerity. It's a form of saying "I realize I made errors. I'm not perfect. There are things I could try to do better." The fact that a term like that has come to be viewed as part of some unsophisticated, retrograde morality that comes from without and disempowers a person is the tragedy of our age. It's why we need to emerge from that materialist age, because that materialist age has nothing but ego to fall back on, and ego is just not enough to live a happy, fulfilled life.

Four Giant Steps for Mankind

Variations of mindfulness-based cognitive therapy, referred to by Jeffrey Schwartz as the Four Steps program, have been successfully used by practitioners to treat a wide range of conditions, including obsessive-compulsive disorder, overeating, gambling, depression, sexual addiction and others. In essence, the program seeks to change the way people think about their thoughts. It rejects the materialist premise that "humans are essentially nothing more than fleshy computers spitting out the behavioral results of some inescapable neurogenetic program," writes Schwartz. So how does it work?

The first step is to *relabel* the problem. Recognize obtrusive, unwanted thoughts or urges for what they are: false signals as opposed to valid ideas that warrant consideration or action.

Step two is to *reattribute* the unwanted thoughts to a flawed brain mechanism. Your thoughts don't have to be *you;* you're not a passive bystander.

The third step is to actively *refocus* your attention away from the wrong thoughts and concentrate on something positive or constructive.

Step four is to *revalue* the problematic thoughts: realize that they have no intrinsic value and no inherent power. As one of Schwartz's patients put it, such thoughts are "toxic waste from my brain."

In large part the program comes down to personal choice and effort, concepts that the materialist view rejects. Schwartz points out, "The teachings of faith have long railed against the perils of the materialist mind-set. . . . The science emerging with the new century tells us that we are not the children of matter alone, nor its slaves."

Finding
Peace of Mind

How can we cope with the distress of daily life to achieve lasting tranquility and peace of mind?

After the most progressive and destructive century in history, it's become a cliché to say that we are living in extraordinary times. Despite the modern miracles that technology has provided, we are living through times of great stress—personally, nationally and globally.

How do we cope with our anxiety about the conditions around us, about personal problems, about the society our children will inherit? Most of us worry but don't know what to do. How do we keep a sense of perspective?

There *is* a way to manage the turbulence that confronts us. There are answers that are effective and encouraging, particularly when we face circumstances that have the potential to paralyze us emotionally: the unexpected loss of a job, the death of a loved one, a failed or failing marriage, feelings of betrayal, health problems. Troubles like these can produce prolonged distress. For the individual caught up in such distress, coping is arduous and painful.

Without oversimplifying or minimizing such traumas, we can be assured that there is a way to find peace of mind—a quiet, calm mental state that is not subject to constant anxiety when pressures build. Many look to self-help to provide the solutions. Although the techniques and devices promoted in popular books and tapes on the subject of managing stress and finding peace may provide a measure of relief, none addresses the fundamental deficiency of the human spirit. To solve our deepest problems we must do better than reprogram our subconscious or learn the latest relaxation techniques.

Seeing the Invisible

The answers that bring lasting solutions are spiritual in nature and derive from the principles involved in exercising godly faith. But before we can exercise faith in God, we need to know that He exists and is personally interested in us. As individuals, we need to think of Him as our Father. So the first step to having the peace of mind we yearn for is to establish that God cares for us in all circumstances and that He has a plan for our lives, both now and in the future.

But how can we know that God even exists?

If the apostle Paul were alive today, he might well answer the question as he did in one of his letters more than 1,900 years ago: "For since the creation of the world God's invisible qualities—His eternal power and divine nature—have been clearly seen, being understood from what has been made, so that men are without excuse" (Romans 1:20, New International Version). According to Paul, we are without excuse if we don't recognize God's divine nature and His eternal power in the natural world.

From rugged panoramas to rain forests, the earth fills us with awe. Its seemingly infinite variety is amazing to contemplate and even more difficult to explain in anything but flights of theory and imagination. Whales communicate by underwater sound, but how did they learn? Migrating birds fly thousands of miles and unerringly arrive at the same location year after year. How did they develop such precise guidance systems?

The apostle Paul said that "the living God . . . made the heaven, the earth, the sea, and all things that are in them." The simple belief that God's existence is evident from what we see in nature has all but disappeared in a world that so boldly proclaims humanity's accomplishments. Yet that childlike trust is the starting point for a right relationship with our Father.

But even if we know that He exists, how can we be sure He cares?

If the creation can teach us something of His existence, perhaps it can teach us something about His concern for us as well.

Tried by Fire

In the shade of the giant sequoias of California, there's a special kind of beauty. These magnificent trees have a tranquility and a majesty that belong to nature alone. They capture our attention, not only for their size but also for their longevity. Some have stood for centuries and bear witness to all the disorder of the past 2,000 years or so.

For example, the General Grant tree is 267 feet (81 meters) tall and 107 feet (33 meters) around the base. Many years ago, a fire scarred the General Grant, leaving an A-shaped gash in its trunk, but the tree survived and continues to grow.

Nearby is an even more startling example of growth despite the adversity of fire. The inside lower half of that tree has been almost completely burned out, yet the top continues to thrive.

Fashioned with loving care, these monuments to God's power testify to the fact that we can, when "fire" strikes us, do more than survive: we can continue to grow.

That understanding begins with the simple belief that our Father has made us with the same care and attention that He gave to the rest of His creation. What is more, He cares for us above everything else He created. Jesus explained this fundamental truth, as recorded in Matthew 6: "Therefore I say to you, do not worry about your life, what you will eat or what you will drink; nor about your body, what you will put on. Is not life more than food and the body more than clothing? . . . So why do you worry about clothing? Consider the lilies of the field, how they grow: they neither toil nor spin. . . . Now if God so clothes the grass of the field, which today is, and tomorrow is thrown into the oven, will He not much more clothe you, O you of little faith?" (verses 25–30).

Paul also spoke of our Father's concern for us. He said that God "allowed all nations to walk in their own ways. Nevertheless He did not leave Himself without witness, in that He did good, gave us rain from heaven and fruitful seasons, filling our hearts with food and gladness" (Acts 14:16–17). In other words, He supplies our needs.

These passages speak to a relationship between the Creator and His creation that is both simple and profound. It is based on a quality of trust that we don't hear much about in our sophisticated high-tech world. Yet that simple trust is the basis of a faith that assures us God will use His power to intervene for our well-being.

God's intervention requires that we have our priorities in the correct order. "Do not worry," Jesus instructed, "saying, 'What shall we eat?' or 'What shall we drink?' or 'What shall we wear?' For the pagans run after all these things, and your heavenly Father knows that you need them. But seek first his kingdom and his righteousness, and all these things will be given to you as well. Therefore do not worry about tomorrow, for tomorrow will worry about itself. Each day has enough trouble of its own" (Matthew 6:31–34, NIV).

Since there is enough to be concerned about on a daily basis, our Father does not want us to be overanxious about our future needs. What we need today, He will provide in answer to prayer, based on belief. He does expect, however, that we will plan for the future, set goals, and then commit those things to Him in prayer.

No Doubt!

Prayer is an important component of godly faith—a vital step in the search for peace of mind. But when we pray, we can expect an answer only when we pray in faith.

The apostle James said: "If any of you lacks wisdom, let him ask of God, who gives to all liberally and without reproach, and it will be given to him. But let him ask in faith, without doubting, for he who doubts is like a wave of the sea driven and tossed by the wind. For let not that man suppose that he will receive anything from the Lord; he is a double-minded man, unstable in all his ways" (James 1:5–8).

The book of Hebrews completes the thought when it says that without faith it is impossible to please God, because anyone who comes to Him must believe that He exists and that He rewards those who earnestly seek Him (Hebrews 11:6).

Tranquility through answered prayer depends on wholehearted belief in God's capacity and willingness to answer.

Another key to gaining peace of mind is to learn what God requires of us and then to act upon that knowledge. This means coming to know God's revealed way of life—discovering how He would live if He were a human being. Jesus Christ's life on this earth is both the representation and the revelation of how our Father would live as a human and how He wants us to live. The source of that revelation, the Bible, teaches us what we need to know to come into sync with God's plan for us.

In the Hebrew Scriptures, the prophet Micah provides the answer to the immediate question of what God requires. He wrote, "He has shown you, O man, what is good; and what does the LORD require of you but to do justly, to love mercy, and to walk humbly with your God?" (Micah 6:8). These are direct instructions for those who seek a genuine relationship with God.

Can I Help You?

As Micah pointed out, God's blessings and protection are available to those who demonstrate justice, selflessness and humility toward their fellow human beings. And although we see very few examples of that kind of high moral conduct, occasionally there are those who act selflessly to right a wrong or extend a kindness to lift others up.

In 2000, heavy rains inundated portions of Zimbabwe, the Republic of South Africa and Mozambique. In the impoverished country of Mozambique alone, an estimated one million people were displaced when the Limpopo River flooded its banks.

South African rescue teams worked tirelessly, often at peril to their own lives, to save those who could be saved. One of the most dramatic efforts reported was the rescue of Sofia and Rositha Pedro—a mother and her newborn daughter. The young woman was one of about a dozen people who had sought refuge in a tree three days earlier when the rising floodwaters forced them from their homes. The rescue occurred about an hour after Rositha was born in that tree, but first a medic from the South African Defense Force had to be brought back from the base camp and winched into the tree by helicopter to cut the umbilical cord.

Other nations also provided help in the rescue efforts, and many, including Britain, Germany, the Netherlands, Norway, Spain and the United States, were involved in ongoing relief work.

There are a number of remarkable aspects to this story in the light of Micah's instructive words. First is the humility that enables people to forget national boundaries, racial differences and perhaps personal or national prejudices to assist others in their time of need. Second is the tenderheartedness that allows people to give of themselves for those who have no foreseeable ability to return the kindness. Third is the respect for the value of another's life, even at the risk of losing one's own. Such an approach is the beginning of understanding where we fit in God's plan for His creation.

In order to act justly, to love mercy, and to walk humbly before our Creator, we have to be willing to give of ourselves for others. In that frame of mind—one in which we see others as being equal in importance to or of greater importance than ourselves—we are freed from anger, malice and a desire for vengeance. And we have the beginning of a proper perspective on ourselves.

Imagine what a different world it would be if the principles addressed by Paul in the first few verses of Philippians 2 were applied consistently and, in particular, in any area that might involve ethnic violence and bigotry. Paul wrote: "Let nothing be done through selfish ambition or conceit, but in lowliness of mind let each esteem others better than himself. Let each of you look out not only for his own interests, but also for the interests of others" (verses 3–4).

Applying such principles isn't easy. But God will help us here as well if we want it and ask for it. It is possible to express the love of God toward our fellow human beings. It is possible to act justly toward one another. And it is also possible to walk humbly with our God, not just with respect to our fellow humans but with respect to Him as well.

Knowing Our Place

Three thousand years ago, King David of Israel addressed our position with respect to that of our Creator. He said: "When I consider your heavens, the work of your fingers, the moon and the stars, which you have set in place, what is man that you are mindful of him, and the son of man that you care for him?" (Psalm 8:3–4, NIV).

Looking at the night sky unassisted by the powerful telescopes we use today, David was humbled by the magnificence of what he saw. Our increased ability to see should produce increased humility and help us to appropriately fix our position within God's creation. If we do, we will not take ourselves too seriously.

In the midst of a titanic personal struggle with loss and despair, the biblical figure Job spoke about God without real understanding. God's response was to question him: "Where were you when I laid the foundations of the earth? Tell Me, if you have understanding. Who determined its measurements? Surely you know! Or who stretched the [measuring] line upon it? To what were its foundations fastened? Or who laid its cornerstone, when the morning stars sang together, and all the sons of God shouted for joy?" (Job 38:4–7).

Lacking answers, Job admitted his insignificance before God. "I know that You can do everything," he said, "and that no purpose of Yours can be withheld from You. . . . I have uttered what I did not understand, things too wonderful for me, which I did not know. . . . I have heard of You by the hearing of the ear, but now my eye sees You. Therefore I abhor myself, and repent in dust and ashes" (Job 42:2–6).

Job had located his place in the order of things. His sense of his own insignificance before God gave him a framework for his life—as a recognition of our own insignificance before God can for us. Despite the fact that humility is the way ahead, and despite its therapeutic benefits for us all, true humility is not something we humans experience very often.

However, when we do, we can come to the kind of peace of mind the apostle Paul had when he wrote: "I have learned in whatever state I am, to be content: I know how to be abased, and I know how to abound. Everywhere and in all things I have learned both to be full and to be hungry, both to abound and to suffer need. I can do all things through Christ who strengthens me" (Philippians 4:11–13). Paul's humility enabled him to express genuine confidence in

God's control over creation, including human life, no matter the circumstances.

A Change of Heart

If we know that God exists and that He cares for us, and we know what He requires of us but fail to act upon it, peace of mind will elude us. Without a proper relationship with Him, the void in the human spirit, which is responsible for so much anxiety and distress, goes unfilled. A proper relationship with God requires that our way of life conform to His. When it does not, the Bible says we are in a state of sin. And our sins act as a barrier between God and us.

Isaiah 59:1–2 tells us that "the arm of the LORD is not too short to save, nor his ear too dull to hear. But your iniquities [or your lawlessness] have separated you from your God; your sins have hidden his face from you, so that he will not hear" (NIV). Our sins—that is to say, living in a way that is contrary to God's teaching—cause Him to turn away from us.

So what is the answer to this dilemma? Is there a way back into God's favor? This same book of Isaiah gives the answer in chapter 1, where it says: "'Come now, and let us reason together,' says the LORD. 'Though your sins are like scarlet, they shall be as white as snow; though they are red like crimson, they shall be as wool'"(verse 18).

God asks us to analyze our lives in the light of His law. That kind of reasoning should produce deep sorrow in us, because we come to see ourselves and our actions from His perspective. More than mere regret, Godly sorrow should produce a complete change on our part so that we begin to live in harmony with His teaching and instruction.

When we do decide to change, God is able to give of Himself for us and act on our behalf. The Bible calls this process repentance, and it is necessary if we are to avail ourselves of the forgiveness made available through Jesus Christ. Repentance and forgiveness are at the beginning of the road to peace of mind. The prophet Isaiah wrote that God "will keep him in perfect peace, whose mind is stayed on [God], because he trusts in [Him]" (Isaiah 26:3).

Transcendent Peace

Learning to trust God implicitly for everything is one of life's great lessons, and it can take a lifetime to accomplish. The guidelines we follow are embodied in the Ten Commandments as amplified by Jesus Christ's teaching in the Sermon on the Mount (Matthew 5, 6 and 7). This is an outline, not of religion, but of a way of life. More than a once-a-week philosophical pacifier, it shows us how we should do business, how to treat our spouses and raise our children, and how to treat coworkers, employers, employees and neighbors. It shows us how to deal with everything that life throws at us, including the inevitable traumas.

If we believe that God cares deeply for us, and that He is willing to use His vast power to intervene on our behalf when He sees a willingness in us to conform our lives to His on the basis of that belief, we can have a peace of mind that defies ordinary human explanation and transcends all human understanding—because it is of God.

The apostle Paul wrote about this: "Do not be anxious about anything, but in everything, by prayer and petition, with thanksgiving, present your request to God. And the peace of God, which transcends all understanding, will guard your hearts and your minds in Christ Jesus" (Philippians 4:6–7, NIV).

This is your path to a quiet spirit, to a mind free of troublesome worry.